judaism

judaism

DANIEL WOOL

Marshall Cavendish Benchmark • 99 White Plains Road • Tarrytown, NY 10591-9001 • www.marshallcavendish.us

• Wool, Danny. Judaism / by Daniel Wool. • p. cm. — (World religions) • Summary: "An exploration of the history and origins, basic tenets and beliefs, organization, traditions, customs, rites, societal and historical influences, and modern-day impact of Judaism"—Provided by publisher. Includes bibliographical references and index. • ISBN-13: 978-0-7614-2118-4 8 ISBN-10: 0-7614-2118-1 1. Judaism—History. I. Title. II. Series. • BM155.3.W66 2006 • 296—dc22 2005016932 Series design by Sonia Chaghatzbanian • Photo research by Candlepants, Inc.

Cover photo: Claudia Kunin/Corbis • The photographs in this book are used by permission and through the courtesy of: *The Image Works*: The British Library/HIP, 1, 3, 4–5, 6–7, 17. *Art Media Musee de Cluny/Heritage-Images*: 8, 54. *Corbis*: Michael Kevin Daly, 2; Bettmann,12, 18; Reuters, 30–31, 96–97; Jonathan Torgovnik, 36; Richard T. Nowitz, 46, back cover; Hanan Isacher, 59; Envision, 62; Roy Morsch, 64–65; Gyori Antoine/SYGMA, 69; Gil Cohen Magen/Reuters, 70–71; Paul A. Souders, 74; Owen Franken, 78; Mark Peterson, 82; Ronan Zvulun/Reuters, 99. *Bridgeman Art Library*: Private Collection/ Archives Charmet, 39–40.

Printed in China • 1 3 5 6 4 2

contents

judaism

The Torah scroll contains the basic teachings of Judaism and the history of the Jewish people. An ornate Torah cover stands to the left.

one

THE EARLY TRADITION

"Hear o israel, the Lord is our god, the Lord is one." For thousands of years this has been the first prayer learned by Jewish children. Some are taught to recite it as soon as they begin to talk, others learn it when they start school, and still others when they begin to prepare for their bar or bat mitzvah ceremonies, when they officially enter the community of Jewish adults. Many recite it in Hebrew, the ancient language of Jewish prayer and learning. Others recite it in English, Russian, Persian, Swedish, or any of the languages that Jews use in their day-to-day lives. Some recite it daily, during morning and evening prayers and just before going to sleep. Others recite it only during holiday services and other special occasions. In one sentence, this prayer, known in Hebrew as the Shema, summarizes the most basic beliefs of the Jewish religion.

This religion, Judaism, is more than three thousand years old. Although Judaism does not have many followers today—there are about 12 to 15 million Jews around the world—it has had an enormous impact on people everywhere. As the oldest of the major monotheistic religions (religions that worship one God), Judaism influenced both Christianity and Islam. Many of the basic beliefs of these religions can be traced to Judaism. Among these are the beliefs that there is one God who created the world and watches over it and who expects each person to act kindly and charitably and to do no harm to any other.

Some of these beliefs are exemplified by a legend that appears in the Talmud, a collection of Jewish laws and folktales collected and edited in the Jewish academies of Israel and Babylonia (modern-day Iraq) about 1,500 years ago. According to the story, a Roman approached Rabbi Hillel and asked to be taught the basics of Judaism while standing on one foot. Hillel smiled and said, "Do not do unto others what you would not have done unto you. This is the law. All the rest is commentary. Go and learn."

Hillel's statement is also the message of the Shema. Since there is only one God who created everyone, no one can claim to be better than anyone else. All people are children of the same God. The sages who wrote the Talmud attempted to understand the Bible, Judaism's most sacred text, and offered many insights into the stories it tells. They asked, "Why did God create only one man and one woman? So that no one can say 'I am better than you, because my ancestors were greater than yours.' After all, we all come from the same ancestors." In other words, all human beings, no matter who they are, where they are from, or what they believe in, are all part of one family, the family of Adam, the first human created by God. As members of that family, people have a responsibility to act kindly and do no harm to one another. This is the message of Judaism.

This same message is shared by Christianity and Islam. What distinguishes Judaism from other religions is the means, rather than the ultimate goal of creating a better world. Jews refer to these means as commandments, or mitzvahs.

According to tradition, there are 613 commandments that appear in the first five books of the Jewish Bible, or the Torah. Of these, 248 are positive commandments, such as "Love thy neighbor" and "Honor thy father and thy mother." The remaining 365 are negative commandments, such as "Thou shall not steal" and "Thou shall not kill." There are commandments about how to observe the many holidays and commandments affecting every stage in a person's life, from waking up in the morning until going to sleep at night, from birth until the moment of death.

No Jew is expected to observe all of these commandments. Some are actually impossible to observe because they relate specifically to events or circumstances that no longer exist in the modern world, such as the commandments regarding the service that was conducted in the ancient Temple in Jerusalem, once the center of all Jewish ritual. Jews believe that by keeping the commandments that are still relevant today, they are helping to make the world a better place, not just for themselves but for people everywhere.

For thousands of years, rabbis and sages have been discussing and debating not only what the commandments mean but also how they can be best observed. While these rabbis and sages might not agree on all points, they are unanimous in their belief that observing the commandments is the most basic ideal of Judaism. This is the Law as explained by Rabbi Hillel.

One of the most important commandments is to study the Torah and all that the rabbis and sages say about it in texts such as the Talmud and in extensive commentaries on the Bible. Study of the Torah is so important that the rabbis asked, "What is preferred? To study the Torah or to perform the commandments?" What is more important: the theory or the practice? As in so many other discussions in the Talmud, the rabbis reached a compromise: "To study is more important, because it leads to action." By studying the commandments and what they mean, people will be better able to perform them. By searching for meaning in the commandments, Jews find clues as to how each commandment helps to make the world a better place. In Jewish tradition, this goal of improving the world is called *tikkun olam* (literally, "mending the world").

What is a Jew? A Jew is a person who believes in one God who created the world and who left a blueprint, the Torah, showing

Some Jews devote their entire lives to studying the teachings of the Torah and its commentaries. The Talmud, which this rabbi is reading, expands on the writings contained in the Torah and is a record of the rabbinic discussions concerning Jewish law, customs, and ethics.

how human beings can continue what God began and be partners in creation by making the world an even better place through acts of justice and the observance of the commandments. It is important to study and understand the Torah to learn how to observe the commandments better.

While Jews consider all people to be part of the same human family, they also believe that they belong to one branch of that family, descended from many of the people mentioned in the Bible. If they were to trace their family trees back far enough, Jews believe that they would find not only Adam but also the biblical patriarchs Abraham, Isaac, Jacob, and one of Jacob's twelve sons, who are the ancestors of the Jewish people. In fact, the word *Jew* itself derives from the name of Jacob's fourth son, Judah. Most Jews with the last names Levy, Levine, Lewin, and Levitt trace their descent to Levi, another son of Jacob. Jews with the name Cohen, Kahn, and Katz usually count Aaron, the brother of Moses, as their ancestor—*Cohen* is the Hebrew word for "priest," and Aaron was the first priest, whose descendants served in the Temple.

According to Jewish tradition, Jews are part of a large family that can be found all around the world, even though they are concentrated in certain areas. This worldwide family is the Jewish people. After many centuries in many different countries, Jews have developed different customs, foods, clothing, and even languages, based on the larger cultures that surrounded them. In many instances, they also found slightly different ways to read and interpret the Torah and its commandments. In the United States today, while most Jews trace their ancestry from Europe, there are also Jews from the Middle East, Africa, India, and Asia. At first glance, they may appear different and have different customs. Nevertheless, they all share the same Torah and follow the same commandments. They believe that they are descended from the same ancestors, the patriarchs: Abraham, Isaac, and Jacob.

The largest group of Jews is the Ashkenazim, who originated in Europe, particularly along the Rhine Valley separating Germany and France. They developed their own language, Yiddish, based on the German dialect spoken there. Over the centuries, the Ashkenazim left their homes to escape persecution and find better opportunities for their families. Most of them gradually made their way to eastern Europe, and from there, many immigrated to North and South America, South Africa, and Australia.

Another large group, the Sephardim, are descendants of Jews who were expelled from Spain by King Ferdinand II and Queen Isabella in 1492, the same year that Christopher Columbus set sail for the New World. A few years later, the Jews of neighboring Portugal were also expelled from their homes and joined the Jews from Spain in exile. The Sephardim settled around the Mediterranean—in North Africa, Greece, Turkey, the Middle East—and in the Netherlands, from where they eventually went to England. Some immigrated to Brazil and the Caribbean. They also developed their own language, Ladino, based on the Spanish and Portuguese they had spoken before the expulsion. The first Jews in what would become the United States were Sephardim who escaped Spain and Portugal and went to Brazil before settling in Dutch New Amsterdam, now the city of New York.

Today, the adjective *Sephardic* is also used to describe many other ancient Jewish communities, such as those of Iraq, Egypt, and Iran, even though most of the Jews in these countries lived there long before they were joined by Jews from Spain. Jews who lived in the Middle East for thousands of years call themselves Mizrahim, "eastern Jews."

There are also much smaller Jewish communities in central Asia, India, Yemen, and Ethiopia. There was once a thriving Jewish community in China, in the city of Kaifeng. Similarly, many Jews from Italy and Greece claim to have been established there for more than two thousand years. They simply call themselves Italian Jews or Greek Jews. Today, no matter where they live, Jews continue to take great pride in the towns and villages where their ancestors once settled. They consider it a badge of pride to be able to say, "I am a Jew from Djerba" (an island off the coast of Tunisia in North Africa), "from Salonika" (a town in northern Greece), or "from Vilna" (the capital of Lithuania).

Jews do not distinguish themselves only by their place of origin. For more than two thousand years, Jews have debated the meaning of the commandments and how best to observe them. In the past, some preferred a literal approach to the Bible and followed the laws exactly as they are written there. Others preferred to allow sages, called rabbis, to interpret the laws in many different ways.

For example, one of the most famous laws in the Bible is called *lex talionis*, based on a verse in the book of Exodus (21:24 or chapter 21 verse 24), which describes what to do if one person injures another: "Eye for eye, tooth for tooth, hand for hand, foot for foot." Thus, the punishment for poking out someone's eye is to have the eye of the offender poked out. Two thousand years ago, the rabbis pointed out that this punishment was particularly harsh and did nothing to help the victim. Instead, they interpreted the Torah to mean that the person who caused the injury should pay the victim the value of that eye. Using assorted verses, they came up with a formula to calculate the exact amount, based on actual injury, the pain it caused the victim, the doctor's fees, loss of work, and the embarrassment caused to the person with one eye. These rabbis interpreted the verse to mean something quite different from what it seems to say at first glance.

Sometimes, the interpretations of the rabbis seem to contradict the original intention of the verses in the Torah. There is a story about the rabbis of the Sanhedrin, the Supreme Jewish Court in the first century C.E., who debated whether a certain oven could be used again if it was defiled. All but one of the rabbis voted that the oven could not be used. The one who believed that it could argued furiously with the other rabbis, finding proof after proof to support his position, but they would not be swayed. Finally, he turned to them and said, "If I am right, let a voice from heaven say so." The walls shook, and a voice from heaven declared that he was right. Even God was on his side, but the rabbis would not be convinced. They conferred among themselves and responded with a quotation from the book of Deuteronomy: "For this commandment which I command you this day . . . It is not in heaven, that you should say, 'Who will go up for us to Heaven and bring it unto us?'" (30:11–12). Once God has given the commandments to humanity, it is up to humanity to decide how to interpret them. The story ends with God laughing and saying, "My children have won the argument."

Still, there were always people who disagreed with the rabbi's interpretation of the Torah and its commandments. Just before the Temple was destroyed by the Romans in 70 C.E., the Jews were divided into several factions, among which were the Sadducees and the Pharisees. The Sadducees, consisting mostly of wealthy priests and aristocrats, were literal in their interpretations of the laws, while the Pharisees, who consisted mostly of scholars, craftsmen, and farmers, were more liberal. Their name means "the interpreters [of the Law]."

Debates over interpretation of the Torah appear again and again throughout Jewish history. In modern times, there are four main groups of Jews, each with its own understanding of the Torah and its commandments. Orthodox Jews believe that the Torah is the word of God, handed down from generation to generation, and should be observed exactly as the rabbis described it, from the days of the Temple until today. Of all the groups, Orthodox Jews are the strictest in their observance of the rituals. Like the Orthodox, Conservative Jews

In medieval and Renaissance times, Jewish texts were often produced as elaborately decorated manuscripts, sometimes depicting the artist's vision of what Jerusalem looked like. This ornately decorated panel from Germany highlights the first word of the book of Deuteronomy.

The Torah

The term *Torah* has two meanings, one broad and inclusive and the other specific. In a broad sense, the word *Torah* is used to describe the books of the Jewish Bible, sometimes called the Old Testament by Christians. The Torah consists of twenty-four books—all of which can be found in the Christian Bible, where they are organized slightly differently—divided into three sections: Torah, Prophets, and Writings. The first section, also called Torah, is the most important to Jews. It consists of just five books, known collectively as the Pentateuch, which tradition claims were written by Moses. These books, which describe the earliest history of the world and of the Jewish people and all of the basic mitzvahs, are Genesis, Exodus, Leviticus, Numbers, and Deuteronomy.

Genesis describes the creation of the world and its earliest history, including the story of the Great Flood and of such figures as the three patriarchs: Abraham, Isaac, and Jacob.

Exodus tells the story of Moses, the Exodus of the Israelites from Egypt, and the early wanderings of the Israelites in the Sinai Desert. It also contains many laws, including the Ten Commandments.

Leviticus describes the responsibilities of the priests, which were later carried out in the Temple.

Numbers continues the story of the Israelites as they travel through the desert until they reach the boundaries of the Promised Land of Canaan.

This painting shows Moses receiving the Ten Commandments.

Deuteronomy contains the last will and testament of Moses. Before he died, Moses gathered all the people before him and repeated the major themes of the Torah, making them swear that they would remain loyal to God and fulfill the commandments.

The second section, Prophets, contains the teachings of the prophets and continues the history of the Israelites up until the destruction of the First Temple in 586 B.C.E. This section contains eight books:

Joshua describes the Israelite conquest of Canaan under Moses's successor, Joshua.

Judges describes the first two and a half centuries of Israelite settlement in Canaan. The people are repeatedly conquered by their neighbors as punishment for failing to observe the commandments, until they repent and God sends great military leaders to rescue them.

Samuel tells the story of the prophet Samuel and the two kings he appointed to rule over the Israelites: Saul and David. The book is usually divided into Samuel I and Samuel II.

Kings recounts the history of the Israelite kings, from Solomon, who built the Temple in about 950 B.C.E., to Zedekiah, during whose reign it was destroyed, in 586 B.C.E. This book is also divided into two sections: Kings I and Kings II.

Isaiah was a prophet who lived in the time described in the book of Kings. In the book of Isaiah he warns the people that they will be punished for their sins, but he also consoles them with a vision of how they will be redeemed in the End of Days, a period of peace throughout the world, when the Jews will be free again. The two parts of the book are so different that many scholars think that they were written by two or more different prophets.

Jeremiah and Ezekiel were both prophets who witnessed the destruction of the First Temple by the Babylonians and the exile of the Jews from their homes. Like Isaiah, they warned the people that it was their sinfulness and lack of concern for others that caused God to punish them. Like Isaiah, they also taught that the Jews would one day be a free nation again and that a brighter future was in store for them.

The book of the Twelve Prophets is really twelve short sections of a single book, each written by a minor prophet explaining the significance of historical events from the time of the First Temple until the earliest days of the return from exile and the construction of a Second Temple. This book also includes the story of Jonah, who was swallowed by a great fish when he refused to obey God's commandment to call the people of the city of Nineveh to repent.

The last section of the Torah, Writings, contains poems, proverbs, stories, and history and culminates in the rebuilding of the Temple in Jerusalem. This section contains eleven books.

Psalms contains 150 poems in praise of God, many of which are attributed to King David.

Proverbs is a collection of wise sayings usually attributed to King Solomon.

Job tells the story of a righteous man who was forced to suffer as a test from God. There is a debate in the Talmud whether the book is an account of a real person or a fictional account written to explain why good people suffer in this world.

Song of Songs is an ancient love song, often explained as a metaphor for the relationship between God and the Jewish people.

Ruth is the story of a young widow who decided to join the Jewish people.

Lamentations is a dirge about the destruction of Jerusalem by the Babylonians in 586 B.C.E. The book is usually attributed to the prophet Jeremiah.

Ecclesiastes is a collection of wise sayings and philosophical musings, also usually attributed to Solomon.

Esther is the story of a Jewish woman who became queen of Persia and rescued the Jews from an evil adviser to the king, who sought to have them killed.

Daniel tells the story of a prophet who lived in Babylonia after the destruction of the Temple in 586 B.C.E.

Ezra-Nehemiah, usually counted as one book in the Jewish Bible, is the story of the return to Jerusalem and the rebuilding of the Temple in about 500 B.C.E.

Chronicles contains the entire history in an abridged form, with an emphasis on the stories of the Israelite kings. It is often divided into Chronicles I and Chronicles II.

In its broader sense, the Torah is more than just the books of the Bible. It is the accumulation of study, of ideas, and even of folktales that rabbis and ordinary Jews have developed and passed down through the generations. Many of these discussions were eventually written down in biblical commentaries by rabbis of every generation for the past two thousand years; in the Mishnah, compiled in Israel around the year 200 C.E.; and in the Gemara, a commentary on the Mishnah, which appears in two editions: one compiled in northern Israel in about 400 C.E. and the other compiled in what is now Iraq about 150 years later. The Mishnah and the Gemara together make up the Talmud. There is also a collection of laws and legends, called the Midrash; digests of all the laws in the Talmud, such as the sixteenth-century *Shulchan Aruch* by Rabbi Joseph Karo; and Responsa Literature in which individuals and communities wrote to the great rabbis of their generation asking for advice on how to respond to particular situations. There are philosophical texts in which rabbis pondered God's actions in the world and the meaning of the commandments, collections of stories and legends, and mystical works in which people expressed their desire to understand God and get closer to him. All of these writings are also considered Torah.

believe that the traditional laws and customs should be observed, but they also believe that Judaism continues to evolve and that the rabbis have the authority to interpret the Torah and its laws as they apply to modern circumstances. Reform Jews believe that the laws of the Torah are inspired by God but that it is up to each individual to decide which of them are personally meaningful and should be observed. Reconstructionist Jews emphasize the importance of the community in deciding which laws are meaningful and should be observed and which should be reinterpreted for the modern world. Despite all these differences, Jews everywhere continue to identify with their ancient traditions, the sense of family that connects them, and the belief that by understanding and performing the commandments, or mitzvoth (the plural of mitzvah), they are taking part in *tikkun olam* and helping to make the world a better place for everyone.

two

IN THE SYNAGOGUE

The Talmud tells the story of two brothers who lived as neighbors and shared a field. One brother was married and had many children, the other was single and lived alone. Every year at the harvest season, they would divide their crops equally between them. One night the single brother could not sleep. "I have far more than I need, while my brother has a large family and many mouths to feed." So he climbed out of bed in the middle of the night and took a bundle of crops to his brother's barn.

That same night the married brother could not sleep either. "I have more than my family needs. Why don't I share some of my crops with my brother? He may not have a family, but at least he will be wealthy." Later that night he climbed out of bed and took a bundle of crops to his brother's barn, hoping his brother would not notice.

The next morning, each brother found that he had exactly the same amount of crops as the day before. Night after night, each brother brought a bundle of crops to the other brother's barn. Each morning they woke up to find that they had exactly the same amount of crops as they had the evening before.

One night the two brothers met in the field, each with a bundle of crops slung across his back. When they realized what had been happening, they dropped their bundles and hugged. God, who was watching, smiled and said, "In this place, where there is so much love between two brothers, I will build my house one day." Many years later, King David bought that field to build the Temple.

According to the Bible, God would not allow David to build the Temple because his hands were bloodied from all the wars he had fought. Instead, his son Solomon built the First Temple on that field outside Jerusalem. The name Solomon is derived from the Hebrew word *shalom*, meaning "peace."

For almost a thousand years, the Temple was the center of Jewish ritual. For four and a half centuries, the caste of priests, the *kohanim*, offered sacrifices there on behalf of all the people. After many years, the people began to fight among themselves, arguing and even going to war against one another, until God had enough. He could no longer live among the Jews in his Temple if the people acted so hatefully. Despite all his warning, given through the prophets, the people refused to listen until, in 586 B.C.E., the Babylonian empire under Nebuchadnezzar destroyed the Temple and sent the people into exile.

For half a century, the Jewish people lived in exile in Babylonia, mourning their lost Temple and all the things that they had done to cause it to be destroyed. In the meantime, a new empire, Persia, conquered the Babylonians, and the Persian king Cyrus allowed the Jews to return to their land and rebuild their Temple on the same spot where Solomon's Temple had once stood. It is with this story of new beginnings and new hopes that the Jewish Bible ends.

The story of the Temple does not end here. After many centuries, once again the Jews began acting spitefully toward one another. Once again, God was frustrated with their behavior and decided to punish them. In 70 C.E. after a long civil war and a revolt against the Roman empire, Jerusalem and the Second Temple were destroyed. Large communities of Jews continued living in Israel for at least four centuries after the Romans destroyed the Temple, but the date 70 C.E. marks the beginning of a new period of exile for Jews.

At the time, many Jews wondered about the future of their religion. Even before the Temple was destroyed, however, a handful of sages realized what was happening around them and where it would all lead. The Temple was a very important part of Jewish life, but it was not the only important part. Prayers could take the place of sacrifices, and the synagogue could become a smaller version of the Temple in Jerusalem, where Jews could meet, study, and pray. When the Temple was destroyed, the synagogue became the center of Jewish life. Prayer and the study of Torah replaced sacrifices as the heart of Jewish ritual.

Almost every Jewish community has at least one synagogue. The synagogue can be an elaborate structure with chapels, classrooms, meeting rooms, and events halls, or a tiny room in the basement of a private home. The synagogue is a place where Jews meet to pray, but it also serves an important social function as a place where Jews gather to celebrate and mourn, to learn, and just to get together.

Each community has its own version of the synagogue. In Europe and the United States, Ashkenazi synagogues have chairs or benches arranged in rows, facing in the direction of the ancient Temple. In Sephardic synagogues, the seats are usually arranged in a circle, with the people facing one another. Some synagogues are towering structures. Others are located below ground, in keeping with a verse in the book of Psalms, "From the depths I call to you, God" (Psalms 130:1). Synagogues have been set up outdoors and in tents, on trains, and even in airplanes. Today many synagogues have schools attached to them, where Jewish children learn about their religion and history.

There are also many different names for a synagogue. Reform Jews usually call their synagogue a temple, recalling how it has assumed the role of the ancient Temple. Sometimes the synagogue is called by its Hebrew name, *beit knesset* (literally, "house of assembly," rather than "house of prayer") or by the Yiddish word *shul*. In some Orthodox communities, there is a synagogue with several rooms in which services start as soon as there is a minimum quorum of ten men. These synagogues are called *shteibels*, from the Yiddish word for "booths." A room that is devoted mainly to Torah study but where regular prayer services are also held is usually called a *beit midrash*, or "house of learning."

Despite the differences, there are certain features that most synagogues share, even though none of these features is absolutely necessary for a space to become a synagogue. Anywhere that Jews gather to pray can become a synagogue.

The most prominent of these features is the *Aron Hakodesh*, or Holy Ark. This is really a cupboard, usually set against the wall facing Jerusalem, where the community's Torah scrolls are stored. Torah scrolls are parchment scrolls containing the first five books of the Bible handwritten in Hebrew by a specially trained scribe called a *sofer*. The parchment is wrapped around two wooden rollers to make it easier to unroll.

Because it is such an important object in the synagogue, each Torah scroll is adorned with special coverings and ornaments. In Ashkenazi synagogues, the scrolls are wrapped with elaborate velvet and embroidered garments. Many Torah scrolls have silver breastplates hanging from their rollers and silver and gold crowns resting above them. Some also have a special pointer, or *yad*, so that the person reading the Torah does not have to touch the parchment. In Sephardic synagogues, the Torah scrolls are often placed in ornate silver cases, sometimes with colorful silk handkerchiefs hanging from them. Ashkenazi Jews generally lay the Torah scroll down to read it. Sephardic Jews generally stand it up in its case to read it.

During services, the Torah scroll may be brought out of the Holy Ark and marched through the synagogue in a small procession. Often people come over to the Torah to kiss it. The ornaments and wrappings are then removed, and it is opened and read. After it is read, it is lifted up so that the entire congregation can see the columns of text. Then it is dressed again with all of its ornaments before it is marched back to the Holy Ark in a similar procession.

The Torah is read in the synagogue on Saturday, the Jewish Sabbath, and on Jewish holidays. The reading is divided into portions, called *parshas*, and the whole Torah is read in one year. Many Reform congregations have adopted an older custom of reading shorter portions so that the whole Torah is read over three years. This much older custom is described in the Talmud. On holidays there are special readings about the specific day and how it should be celebrated.

On the Sabbath, the reading is divided into seven smaller sections called *aliyot* (literally, "going up"). A member of the community is called up before each *aliyah* (the singular of *aliyot*) to make a blessing over the Torah before it is read. The reader then chants the words to an ancient melody, highlighting certain key words and adding pauses when necessary. The melody is especially important because the text as written on the Torah scroll contains no vowels and no punctuation. It is just columns of words, with longstanding traditions of how they are to be read. The melody indicates where each verse (called in Hebrew a *pasuk*) ends and what the key phrases are.

While anyone is entitled to chant from the Torah, it requires special training to read the words and chant the melody; so usually one or more readers prepare the sections in advance, learning how to read the words correctly and chant them according to a series of notes called *trope*, which appear in some Hebrew Bibles. This special training is a major part of the studies that Jewish boys and girls go through to prepare for their bar or bat mitzvah, the ceremony at which they come of age before the entire community.

The Talmud describes how in ancient times the Torah was chanted very softly, and a man standing next to the reader would translate the words into Aramaic. In the time of the Second Temple and the Talmud, most Jews living in Israel and Babylonia did not speak Hebrew well enough to follow the text and understand it. The most commonly spoken language was Aramaic, and by reciting aloud the Aramaic translation, called Targum, they were more likely to understand the

Torah reading. Today only a few communities, including some Jewish communities from Yemen, follow this practice.

In the United States each member of the congregation follows the reading in an individual Bible, called a *Chumash* (literally, "the Five," for the five books of Moses that it contains), sometimes with a translation into English written alongside the Hebrew text. Often the *Chumash* has one or more of the traditional Aramaic translations, most notably one called *Targum Onkelos*, named after the Roman convert who supposedly composed it. Ironically, the legend states that Onkelos was a nephew of the emperor Titus, who ordered the attack on Jerusalem that led to the destruction of the Second Temple.

After the Torah is read, a notable member of the community (or the person celebrating a bar or bat mitzvah) is called up to the Torah, and the final few verses of that week's portion are repeated, most likely to show how reluctant Jews are to put away the Torah once they have started to read it. The person who is called to make the blessing over this reading is called a *maftir*, and the word is now used to describe the reading itself. On holidays and several times throughout the year, a special *maftir* is read from another part of the Torah that relates to the occasion.

Once the Torah reading is finished, the person who read the *maftir* reads a chapter from the Prophets, called the haftorah, relating to that week's reading. For example, after reading the opening chapters of the book of Genesis, which describe the creation of the world, it is customary to read from the book of Isaiah (42:5–43:10), since this section begins, "Thus says God the Lord, He that created the Heavens and stretched them out, He that spread forth the Earth and that which comes out of it, He that gives breath unto the people that walk on it, and spirit to them that walk therein." This verse summarizes the story of the creation that was read earlier in the Torah.

Usually, the Torah and haftorah are read from a small stage called a *bimah*, located in the center of the synagogue. In Orthodox and many Conservative synagogues, it is customary to read facing the Holy Ark; in Reform temples and some Conservative synagogues, the *bimah* is located toward the front of the synagogue, and the Torah is read facing the congregation.

The *bimah* is also where the person leading the prayers usually stands during the services. While any member of the congregation can lead the prayers, it is often a trained individual, called a cantor, or *hazan*. The cantor is someone who has studied all the prayers and knows all the melodies that the community uses to sing them. Some of these melodies, like the *trope* used to read the Torah and haftorah, can date back many hundreds of years. Others are more recent and have been influenced by Christian liturgical music, opera, and even pop songs. In some synagogues the cantor is accompanied by a choir, and in many Reform temples, organs, pianos, guitars, and other instruments accompany the service.

Each synagogue may have other furnishings too. Sometimes there is a menorah (candelabrum), to remind worshippers of the menorah that burned constantly in the Temple. Very often, the menorah is represented by a single lamp, called a *Ner Tamid* (eternal light), which hangs in front of the Holy Ark. Some synagogues also have a pulpit for the rabbi to give a weekly sermon. The Holy Ark itself may be covered by a *parochet*, or curtain, which is drawn back to remove the Torah scrolls. While none of these is absolutely essential to the services, they remind worshippers of the sanctity of the space and are usually elaborately decorated.

In Orthodox synagogues, only men lead the services, and men and women sit separately. Sometimes women are seated in a balcony overlooking the main sanctuary, but often they are separated from

When reciting the first verse of the Shema, it is customary to cover the eyes to help concentrate on the meaning of the words. These men have gathered for a convention held in Tel Aviv, Israel.

the men by a barrier or curtain called a *mehitzah*. Conservative and Reform congregations have done away with the *mehitzah*, and women play a more active role in the service, often serving as rabbis and cantors. One of the challenges facing many Orthodox congregations today is to find ways to integrate women more fully into the services without discarding the *mehitzah* or doing away with the traditional responsibilities that men have in the community.

The synagogue can be a busy place every day of the year. Traditionally, Jews pray three times a day: morning, afternoon, and evening. The morning service, or *shacharit*, is the longest; *minchah*, the afternoon service, is very brief (since it often interferes with the workday) and is often recited a few minutes before *ma'ariv*, the evening service, with the time between them sometimes used to study Torah.

Prayers can be recited in any language, though most Orthodox and Conservative Jews recite them in Hebrew. There is a folktale about an orphaned cowherd who did not know how to recite any prayers. It was Yom Kippur, the most solemn day of the Jewish year, and he could not follow the services or even figure out if he should be standing or seated. Suddenly he started to whistle. The outraged elders of the community rushed over to him and grabbed him, shouting, "How dare you make a mockery of the services on this, the holiest of days."

Just as they were about to toss him out of the synagogue, the rabbi ordered them to put the boy down. "Why were you whistling?" he asked him gently.

The boy looked up at the rabbi with tears in his eyes. "Today is Yom Kippur and I wanted God to hear me. I wish I could pray like everyone else, but I can't even read the words, so I thought that if I whistled, maybe God would hear me too."

The rabbi smiled and turned to the community, "All day, I've felt that God was not listening to our prayers. All of that changed when I heard this boy whistle. He was crying out to God with all his heart, and God heard him. Because of this boy, he heard all of you too."

In Judaism, it is the passion rather than the words that make prayer a meaningful experience. Like the young cowherd, however, few people really know how to achieve that high level of passionate communication, one on one, with God; so the rabbis have developed a prayer book called the *siddur*, containing what they consider to be time-tested formulas for reaching God through prayer.

The main prayer in the *siddur* is called the *Shmoneh Esrei*, or Eighteen Benedictions, though it is really a misnomer, since the version recited on weekdays actually contains nineteen benedictions—the nineteenth was added after the prayer was originally composed—and the version recited on the Sabbath and most holidays has only seven. *Shmoneh Esrei* is said while standing and in a whisper, though it is repeated by the cantor for the entire congregation during *shacharit* and *minchah*. The cantor's reading was originally done for the benefit of people who could not read the prayer in the *siddur*, but it has since become such an established custom that it is still repeated today even though most people are literate.

The *Shmoneh Esrei* opens with two blessings praising God for helping humanity both in the past and in the future and one blessing declaring God's holiness. The opening is followed by thirteen blessings asking for God's help in many different ways; included are a prayer for forgiveness, a prayer for health, and even a prayer asking God to answer all people's prayers. The nineteenth prayer, or benediction, which asks God to protect the Jewish people from their enemies, was added at a time of severe persecution and remains today. The final three blessings are similar to the first three in that they are in praise of God, ending with a prayer for peace. A final paragraph asks God to prevent people from speaking ill of others. On Sabbath and holidays, the thirteen middle benedictions are replaced by a single prayer thanking God for granting Jews that day of celebration.

Another important prayer in *shacharit* and *ma'ariv* is the Shema. Apart from the verse "Hear O Israel, the Lord is our God, the Lord is One," the Shema includes three paragraphs: one commands people to love God (Deuteronomy 6:4–9); another describes the rewards for those who keep the commandments: "So that you and your children may live long in the land that God swore to your fathers he would give them" (Deuteronomy 11:13–21); and the third (Numbers 15:37-41) reminds people that God took the Israelites' ancestors out of slavery in Egypt so that they would observe the commandments.

The morning service includes readings from the book of Psalms and other sections of the Bible. On Mondays and Thursdays, the first section of the next week's Torah reading is chanted, and three people are called up to the Torah for an *aliyah*. Each service includes one or more recitations of the Kaddish, a prayer recited by mourners during the eleven months following the death of a parent and for thirty days after the death of other family members. Recited in Aramaic, this prayer makes no mention of the dead and is a series of praises of God. The idea behind it is that even in a time of distress, Jews recognize that God rules the world and acts justly for the good of humanity. The Kaddish ends with a statement: "May he who has created peace in Heaven, grant peace to us and all the Jewish people." Finally, each service ends with an ancient prayer, called *Aleinu*, reminding people of their responsibility to praise God and to engage in acts of *tikkun olam*, to make the world a better place for everyone.

On Sabbath and holidays, a fourth service, called *Musaf*, is recited in Orthodox and Conservative synagogues. The *Musaf*, like all the other *Shmoneh Esreis* recited on Sabbath and holidays, consists of only seven benedictions, with the middle blessing recalling the sacrifices that were once offered in the Temple to celebrate the day. Reform congregations generally do not recite the *Musaf* service.

Another service is the Friday night *Kabbalat Shabbat* (Welcoming the Sabbath), recited between *minchah* and *ma'ariv*, the afternoon and evening services. This very short service includes the reading of six psalms—one for every day of creation—and the singing of a poem, "*Lechah Dodi*," which compares the Sabbath to a bride and calls on the congregation to welcome her. This poem was originally composed by the mystical rabbis of the town of Safad in the hills of northern Israel in the sixteenth century. Rather than sing it in the synagogue, these rabbis and their followers would descend into the nearby fields and valleys, where they would watch the sun set and sing and dance to welcome the Sabbath. There is a custom, while singing the last verse, to turn to the door and bow, while beckoning the Sabbath to enter, saying, "Enter, O bride! Enter, O bride!" The congregation then sings Psalms 92 and 93, in praise of the Sabbath that has just arrived.

There are many traditional garments that Jews wear in the synagogue or whenever they pray. Men, and often women, cover their heads as a sign of respect with either a hat or a small skullcap, called a *kippah* in Hebrew or yarmulke in Yiddish. Reform Jews do not insist on wearing a yarmulke during services, while Orthodox and many Conservative Jewish men (and some women) wear one at all times or at least when they pray, study Torah, and eat. Actually, the Torah has no commandment for wearing a head covering, and it is only hinted at in later sources, such as the Talmud. Nevertheless, the idea of covering one's head as a reminder that God is always watching from above has become so much a part of Jewish custom that the yarmulke is, for many people, a symbol of Jewish pride.

Orthodox men and Conservative and Reform men and women also wear a prayer shawl, or tallith, when they pray. It is a four-cornered garment with a type of macramé fringe, called tzitzit, attached to each corner. Sometimes the tallith is as large as a big towel and covers the head as well as the body. At other times the tallith is more like a scarf that is hung around the neck. Wearing the tallith, unlike the yarmulke, is a way of fulfilling a commandment in the Torah that appears in the third paragraph of the Shema (Numbers 15:38–40): "Speak to the sons of Israel and tell them to put tassels on the hems of their garments." The following verse explains the reason: "This will remind you of all my commandments; put them into practice, and you will be consecrated to your God and not follow after your heart and your eyes, which lead you astray." While most Jews wear a tallith only in the synagogue, many Orthodox and Conservative men wear a smaller, poncholike version under their shirt at all

Some Jews wrap a large tallith around their head and shoulders when praying. This young man attends services at a temple in Queens, New York.

times, to constantly remind them of their responsibilities to God and humanity.

On weekdays during the morning service, many Jewish men also put on tefillin, tiny black leather boxes containing brief portions from the Torah—including the Shema—which they bind to their forehead and the muscle of the weaker arm (not the arm used to write) with leather straps. Wearing the tefillin is also the fulfillment of a commandment in the Shema, "You shall fasten them on your hand as a sign and on your forehead as a circlet" (Deuteronomy 6:8). Tefillin remind Jews that everything they think (the tefillin tied to the head represent thoughts), do (the tefillin tied to the hand represent actions), and feel (the tefillin tied to the arm and pointed to the heart represent emotions) should be directed to serving God by keeping the commandments. They are a reflection of the earlier verse, "You shall love the Lord, your God with all your heart, with all your soul [the mind], with all your strength [the hand]" (Deuteronomy 6:5).

Someone once asked a great rabbi, the Baal Shem Tov, how it was possible for him to keep the commandment to love God with all his heart, his soul, and his might. "After all," the man posing the question reasoned, "God is so great that I cannot even imagine Him! I can understand how I can love my family and I can love my home, but how can I possibly love something that I cannot even see or feel?"

The Baal Shem Tov answered, "It is actually very simple. The Torah, which commands us to love God, also tells us that 'God created man in his own image, in the image of God created he him, male and female created he them' (Genesis 1:27). By loving all people, who are created in God's image, a person is showing his love of God." Loving God by loving humanity is the ideal of Jewish worship, as stated in the Shema and in the teachings of Rabbi Hillel. The prophets and rabbis taught that it was the Jewish people's failure to observe those commandments that teach how to treat people compassionately that led to the destruction of two Temples. Hence, Jewish congregations everywhere try to transform the synagogue into a place of peace where people study, collect charity, and help one another.

The star of David

Many synagogues around the world are decorated with a six-pointed star known as the Star of David, or Magen David in Hebrew (*magen* means "shield"). The Star of David has become so popular that it has come to represent the Jewish people. It can be found on ritual objects, on fabrics, and on jewelry, such as necklaces. During the Holocaust, the Nazis forced Jews to wear a yellow Star of David on their clothing so they could be easily identified. Several years later, a blue Star of David was chosen as the symbol of the State of Israel and placed in the center of that country's flag.

Actually, no one really knows when the Star of David first became associated with the Jewish religion. No explanation has been found so far in archaeological excavations from biblical times in the land of Israel, and the earliest known example of the star's use to decorate a ritual object is on a third-century Jewish tombstone from Italy. In the fourteenth century, the Star of David began appearing on the flags of Jewish communities and shortly thereafter on synagogues, as well as on menorahs, necklaces, and many other objects. In modern times, Jews have used the Magen David as a symbol of pride in their heritage—even if King David himself is likely never to have used it.

This yellow Star of David was worn by a French Jew during the Holocaust as a badge of shame.

three

IN THE HOME

while the synagogue is the focus of the Jewish community, the real center of Jewish life is the home, where many of the most important rituals take place, among family, friends, and guests.

In some ways, Jews try to model their home after the tent of their biblical ancestor Abraham. According to a legend, Abraham's tent was open in four directions so he could always see if any strangers were traveling through the desert and needed his hospitality. The Bible says that when Abraham was already a very old man, he saw three strangers approaching his tent; "he ran from the entrance of the tent to meet them" (Genesis 18:2) and invited them to stay with him. He offered them water to wash themselves and bread to eat before running off again to prepare a full meal. It is for his hospitality to strangers that Abraham is so loved by Jews. He exemplifies the commandment of *hachnasat orchim*, or welcoming guests into the home.

One of the first things guests see when entering a Jewish home is a mezuzah, a little rectangular box, nailed to the right doorpost of the main entrance and almost every doorway. It can be a simple plastic container or an elaborate piece of art made out of porcelain or precious metals. Inside the box is a tiny parchment scroll inscribed with the first two paragraphs of the *Shema*. (Deuteronomy 6:4–9 and 11:13–21). This scroll is the fulfillment of the commandment "Write them on the doorposts of your houses and your gates" (Deuteronomy 11:20). It is as if a miniature Torah scroll were attached to the door of every room, reminding people that this home is dedicated to fulfilling the commandments.

In many private homes, a small section of wall often is left unfinished, without any plaster or paint. This ancient custom not only reminds the people living there of the destruction of the Temple, but it is also a statement that no home can ever be complete. Jews have a constant responsibility to strive to make the home and the world a better place for everyone.

One of the most important rooms in the house is the kitchen. Food and the rituals surrounding meals have always been an important part of Jewish life, and there are many laws and customs about how it is to be prepared and eaten. The laws for preparing food are called kashruth, and food prepared according to these laws is called kosher.

These laws do not mean that Jews can eat only "Jewish foods." In fact, a common Jewish food like a bagel will be as exotic as *cuscus* (a type of grain) to a Moroccan Jew or *ndjara* (a type of bread) to an Ethiopian Jew. Jews have always adapted the foods of their native countries to the laws of kashruth, and so Jewish cuisine encompasses recipes from virtually every country of the world. While these recipes tend to follow the laws of kashruth, many Jews no longer eat only kosher food or eat kosher only at home. Nevertheless, kashruth is the basis of Jewish recipes, and it is still strictly observed by Orthodox Jews as well as many Conservative Jews.

The laws of kashruth are derived from the Bible, though they have evolved considerably over the centuries and are now rather complicated. Perhaps the best-known law is the prohibition against eating pork, although the Bible lists many other animals that may not be eaten (see, for instance, Leviticus 11), including horse, camel, rabbit, and all shellfish. Only certain mammals and birds may be eaten, though some species of locusts are also permitted. Mammals must have split hooves, which is why horse meat is forbidden, and they must chew their cud (regurgitate and redigest their food), which is why pork is forbidden. No predatory mammals or birds are allowed.

Jews who observe kashruth will not eat meat that has been hunted. In order to be eaten, the animal must be slaughtered according to an ancient technique called *shechitah*. This procedure requires the use of a special knife, called a *halaf,* which is run across the animal's carotid and jugular veins with a single stroke. Death occurs in seconds with minimal pain. The knife must be especially sharp so that the animal does not feel the cut; some kosher butchers, called *shochets*, have a custom of running the knife across their finger to see if they feel any pain. The blood that is drawn is covered by earth, out of respect for the animal.

Since the laws of kashruth forbid the consumption of blood, the meat is carefully rinsed and salted. Some organs, such as liver, which contain more blood, are eaten only after they have been roasted over an open flame to remove any remaining blood.

Only fish that have fins and scales are permitted. Thus shark, catfish, and eels are forbidden. Similarly, all shellfish, including lobster, shrimp, calamari, and oysters, is not kosher. There are no laws as to how fish must be killed before they are eaten.

The laws of kashruth also divide food into three distinct categories: meat (*basar* in Hebrew, *fleischig* in Yiddish), dairy (*chalav* in Hebrew, *milchig* in Yiddish), and pareve, or neutral, foods, which include grains, fruits, vegetables, and eggs. Traditionally, Jews will not eat any meat products with dairy products. Though this practice is not commanded explicitly in the Torah, it derives from the commandment "You shall not boil a kid in its mother's milk," which appears three times in the Bible (Exodus 23:19 and 34:26; Deuteronomy 14:21). As it is repeated word for word, the rabbis interpreted the commandment to mean meat and dairy should never be cooked or served together; meat includes fowl but not fish.

Because of this commandment, many Jewish homes have separate plates and cutlery for meat and dairy; some homes will even have two sinks. It is also customary to wait after eating meat before eating dairy so the food is digested separately. Dutch Jews wait only one hour, German Jews wait three hours, while other Jews wait six hours.

Despite all these restrictions, Jewish cooks have devised many clever ways to prepare and serve delicious meals. Even after a meat meal, coffee can be served with nondairy creamer, and there are pareve substitutes, made from tofu and other vegetable products, for all sorts of dairy foods, including ice cream and cheesecake.

While Jews believe that the laws of kashruth apply only to themselves, there is one important commandment regarding food that applies to all people everywhere. According to the Torah, there are seven commandments, called the Seven Noachide Laws, that are the basis of a civilized society and that apply to everyone regardless of their religion. One of these, called *ever min ha-chai*, forbids people to eat the limb of any living animal. Avoiding all cruelty to animals is an important law of the Torah, and Jews are even commanded to feed their animals before they feed themselves.

It may seem surprising that Jews are not vegetarians. In fact, many Jews, including many prominent rabbis, are, and they often quote a verse from the Bible: "See, I give you all the seed-bearing plants that are upon the whole earth, and all the trees with seed-bearing fruit; this shall be your food" (Genesis 1:29). According to God's original plan, they claim, all of humanity should have been vegetarian. The passion to eat meat, however, was too strong to overcome, and so God placed restrictions on meat eating to force people to think about what they are doing before they slaughter an animal and eat it.

Another commandment tells Jews not to waste any food or for that matter any other products. Tossing good food into the garbage or wasting paper is a violation of the commandment of *bal tashchit*, and many Jews today treat recycling as a mitzvah.

Jews believe it is important to show gratitude for the food they have. Even a slice of bread or a glass of clean water can make the difference between life and death for children in famine-stricken countries. To show their gratitude, many Jews recite a brief prayer, called a *brachah*, or blessing, before they eat anything. There are special *brachot* (the plural of *brachah*) for fruit, vegetables, products made of grain, bread, and wine—all foods that are pareve. For all other foods the *brachah* is "Blessed are you, Lord our God, who has created everything."

Before a meal or even before eating bread, traditional Jews often wash their hands by pouring water over them from a cup or pitcher in imitation of the way that priests prepared themselves to eat the food offerings in the Temple. Like the synagogue, the home itself is a small temple, and the table where people eat is often compared to the altar. Thus, all knives are removed from the table when reciting the special blessings after eating, called Grace after Meals, or *Birkat HaMazon*. The home, like the temple, is supposed to be a place of peace, and knives are symbols of violence.

There is a story about Rabbi Judah ha-Nasi, a leader of the Jewish people and the editor and compiler of the Mishnah, who was on very friendly terms with the Roman emperor. One day, he invited the emperor to be his guest in his home for dinner. All that day, the rabbi and his family prepared the finest foods, which they served on their best dishes. The emperor enjoyed the meal so much that he was determined to come back again a few days later. He even requested that the exact same foods be served so that he could recapture the wonderful time he had had at the meal.

A few days later the emperor returned. Again the rabbi and his family had spent the day preparing the meal, and the table was set exactly as it had been the previous time. Although the emperor enjoyed the food and company, this meal was not quite as enjoyable to him as the previous one. He decided to tell Rabbi Judah what he had experienced.

The rabbi thought for a moment and responded. "Your Majesty is right, of course. You see, last time we added a special seasoning to the meal, which we could not add today."

"A seasoning?" the emperor wondered. "You must tell me what it is so that I can buy it for my cooks to use in all my food!"

"No," answered Rabbi Judah, "because that seasoning is the Sabbath day, which makes everything more pleasurable."

Once a week, every week, Jews gather in their homes to celebrate the Sabbath. While there are special prayers and services in the synagogue, the Sabbath is really a celebration for friends and family in the home. Over one hundred years ago, a Jewish thinker named Ahad Ha'am wrote, "More than Israel has kept the Sabbath, the Sabbath has kept them." Abraham Joshua Heschel, a prominent American rabbi and civil rights activist, referred to the Sabbath as a "palace in time."

Called *Shabbat* in Hebrew and *Shabbos* in Yiddish, the Sabbath is a time for Jews to stop everything that keeps them busy day after day and celebrate the simple things that really matter but that are often taken for granted. It is not only a day of rest, it is also a celebration of creation, a day for basking in what already exists.

According to the rabbis, there are two distinct commandments associated with the Sabbath: to remember and celebrate the day and to observe it by refraining from any creative work. The Sabbath commemorates two major events in the history of the world: the end

Jews light two candles on Friday night to mark the beginning of the Sabbath.

of creation, when God rested, and the liberation of the Israelite slaves from Egypt and the beginning of their march toward freedom.

The Sabbath begins on Friday night at sunset with the lighting of two candles commemorating the two commandments: to remember and to observe. Some people light a candle for each member of their immediate family.

Today, the lighting of candles is identified with the Sabbath: many Jewish families who observe little else continue to light candles every Friday night. This custom was not originally part of the celebration and is not mentioned in the Torah. There is, however, a distinct commandment not to light any fires on the Sabbath. Unfortunately, people ended up sitting in the dark, bumping into each other, and even spilling food on the people they were trying to serve. The result was often fighting and discord among family members. As one of the goals of the Sabbath was to create *shalom bayit*, (peace in the home), the rabbis decreed that every family should light candles so that there is light—and peace—in the home. This practical ritual resolved a common problem.

After attending the service in the synagogue, the family gathers in the home for a festive meal. The table is set with a white tablecloth in remembrance of the manna that God provided as food for the Israelites while they wandered in the desert for forty years after leaving Egypt. The best china and silverware are used.

According to an old folk legend, two angels enter the home every Sabbath as the family sits down to eat to see whether everything is ready. If it is, one angel says, "May every Sabbath be as peaceful as this," and the other angel says, "Amen." If nothing is ready, the second angel says, "May every Sabbath be as peaceful as this," and the first angel must answer, "Amen."

To welcome these angels, the family sings *Shalom Aleichem*, a hymn that greets them and asks them to bless the home. In some traditional homes, the husband then sings the last chapter of the book of Proverbs to his wife (Proverbs 31:10–31), which describes a "virtuous woman."

The meal begins with a prayer called kiddush over a goblet of red wine or grape juice. Kiddush literally means "sanctification." Reciting the kiddush sanctifies the day and declares it different from all other days. Wine is used to show that this celebration is a happy event. After the prayer is recited, everyone sips from the goblet.

The meal begins with two loaves of braided bread, called challah, sometimes sweetened with raisins. The two loaves represent the double portion of manna that the Israelites received in the desert every Friday so that they would not have to gather food on the Sabbath. Before it is served, the bread is usually sprinkled with salt. Salt was offered with all the sacrifices in the Temple, and the table is compared to the altar.

Since many traditional families do not watch television or go out on Friday night, the meal is usually a leisurely affair, accompanied with stories and special Sabbath songs called *zemirot*. Many of the songs are hundreds of years old, though new tunes are always being composed. The meal ends with Grace after Meals.

From sunset on Friday evening until Saturday night, many Jews will not perform any creative work, called *melachah* in Hebrew. The rabbis who compiled the Talmud counted thirty-nine separate *melachot* (plural of *melachah*) that should not be performed on the Sabbath, except those needed to save a life, but over the centuries, many more common tasks have been included. For instance, it is forbidden to write on the Sabbath; so the rabbis enacted a special restriction that people should not even carry a pen, since they might forget that it is the Sabbath and write something down. Objects that may not be carried are called *muktzeh*.

Other work prohibited on the Sabbath includes gardening, painting, sewing, lighting or putting out fires (in ancient times, this task required considerable effort), and cooking. Families usually prepare all of the food for Sabbath in advance, often on Friday. To make sure there is a hot meal on Saturday, Jewish cooks have developed all sorts of special recipes that can be put on the stove on Friday afternoon to cook all night. The most famous of these is *chulent*, a hot stew made of meat, beans, potatoes, barley, and just about anything else that people feel like tossing in it. The original recipe for *chulent* is at least a thousand years old. The name most likely comes from two French words: *chaud*, meaning "hot," and *lent*, meaning "slow." The stew cooks slowly to provide a hot meal for Saturday lunch.

Chulent is popular all over Europe, North America, and North Africa, where it is called *hamin*. In Yemen, Jews often prepare special breads called *kubaneh* and *jahnoun*, which bake all night. While these foods can be eaten any day of the week, as the emperor discovered at Rabbi Judah ha-Nasi's house, they taste especially good on the Sabbath when shared with family and guests.

On Saturday itself, there are usually services in the synagogue in the morning, followed by another festive meal with wine and two loaves of bread. After the meal, Jews love to take a long nap to sleep off the heavy *chulent*, and get refreshed for the week to come. In the late afternoon, there is a third, light meal called *seudah shlishit* (literally, "the third meal"), during which Jews say their good-byes to the departing Sabbath with slow songs.

The Sabbath ends at nightfall with a ceremony called *havdalah*. This is a brief prayer, often recited in the home, over a goblet of wine. During the ceremony, a special candle is lit, to represent the fact that Jews are once again permitted to do work and light fires and also in commemoration of the first act of creation described in chapter 1 of Genesis: the creation of light. Many Jews have a custom of examining their fingernails by the light of the candle to show that they are actually

Judaism is not a religion that seeks converts. In Jewish tradition, all people, regardless of their religion, can have a direct relationship with God, provided that they act morally and do no harm to others.

To explain this outlook, Jews relate a story that appears in the play *Nathan the Wise* by the German playwright Gotthold Lessing. According to the story, the emperor Saladin once asked an elderly Jew named Nathan the Wise to tell him what the true religion is. Nathan responded with the tale of a ring that was passed down from generation to generation from father to favorite son. Finally, there was a father who loved each of his three sons equally and could not decide to which of them he would give the ring. So he had a jeweler make two identical copies of it. As he lay on his deathbed, he called in each son, one at a time, gave him a ring and made him swear not to show it to the other brothers until he had died.

When the brothers realized what had happened, they quarreled bitterly over who had the real ring. It took a wise judge to resolve their predicament. He advised each brother to act as if his ring was the original so they would all live up to their father's expectations.

In Judaism, these expectations are that everyone must live a moral life according to seven basic rules that are shared by all religions:

1. **Do not murder.**

2. **Do not steal.**

3. **Do not worship false gods (this rule can also be interpreted to mean the self, money, or any other thing that people sometimes place above the welfare of others).**

4. **Do not commit adultery.**

5. **Do not eat the limb of an animal that is still living (generally interpreted as Do not be cruel to animals).**

6. **Do not curse God.**

7. **Establish courts to mete out justice fairly to all.**

By following these laws, Jews believe that every person is taking part in the ideal of *tikkun olam* and is making the world a better place.

benefiting from the light. On Friday night, separate candles were lit to mark the beginning of the Sabbath. During *havdalah*, a braided candle is used to represent how everyone has become closer during the Sabbath.

A blessing is also made over fragrant herbs or spices. According to an ancient mystical tradition, Jews celebrating the Sabbath receive an extra soul on that day, but that soul departs once the Sabbath is over. The spices serve as smelling salts to revive everyone after losing that Sabbath soul. By the time Sunday rolls around, Jews everywhere are already planning what they can do to make the next Sabbath even more restful and meaningful.

In modern times, Jews observe the Sabbath in many different ways. Some will not speak on the phone or travel, while others will. Some will spend more time in the synagogue than others. What unites Jews, however, is the idea that one day every week, they can escape from the hustle and bustle of a hectic world to take pleasure in the things that really matter to them, like family and friends or just looking at the flowers in a garden without trying to control the way they grow. By not running out to shop or catch a movie, they have a chance to appreciate everything they have around them, no matter how mundane and simple. Perhaps that is what Ahad Ha'am meant when he said: "More than Israel has kept the Sabbath, the Sabbath has kept them."

four

THE JEWISH CALENDAR

If elderly Jews are asked about something that happened long ago, they will often answer by referring to one of the Jewish holidays: "one week before Rosh Hashanah" or "three days after Passover." The cycle of holidays sets the rhythm for the Jewish year, and holiday preparations often begin weeks in advance with the compiling of guest lists and menu planning. Like the Sabbath, most Jewish holidays are celebrated around the dining room table in the home in the company of family and friends.

Most of the Jewish holidays and their rituals are described in the first five books of the Bible. Many holidays commemorate historical events, particularly events associated with the Exodus of the Israelites from Egypt. Others coincide with agricultural events in the land of Israel, such as the different harvest seasons. In biblical times most Jews were farmers, and the harvest was a time for celebration and thanksgiving.

The first holiday of the year is Rosh Hashanah, the Jewish New Year, which occurs over two days in early autumn. It is a solemn holiday, but it is also a celebration. It is a time for Jews to reflect on all that they have done over the past year and apologize to anyone they insulted or hurt. Making amends with people who have been hurt is the first act of repentance and often the most difficult.

For example, gossip is considered to be a serious sin in Judaism, since the damage that it causes is so hard to repair. There is a story about a student who went to his rabbi on the day before Rosh Hashanah and asked the rabbi for forgiveness for spreading some mean stories. The rabbi agreed to forgive him on the condition that the student take a feather pillow, slice it open, and let the feathers scatter in the wind. "After you collect them all," the rabbi continued, "you will be forgiven."

"But that's impossible!" the student stammered. "How can I possibly find them all?"

"It's the same with gossip," the rabbi answered. "Once you've let it out into the wind, you can never collect it all back again."

It can be very difficult to make amends, but another commandment holds that if a person is sincere in asking for forgiveness, that person must be forgiven.

Rosh Hashanah is also a time to begin the process of asking God to forgive all those mistakes for which there is no one to ask for forgiveness. In the Jewish tradition, there are three things that can be done to receive God's forgiveness: *teshuvah*, or repentance, expressing remorse for one's mistakes; *tefillah*, or prayer, asking forgiveness directly from God; and *tzedakah*, or giving charity, which shows a sincere desire to make the world a better place.

To arouse the congregation to consider their trangressions and mistakes, a ram's horn, or shofar, is blown in the synagogue during Rosh Hashanah services. The shofar is an ancient instrument that dates to the earliest days of the Bible. Its three notes are compared to the sound of someone crying: a long wail, called *tekiah*; three shorter sobs, called *shevarim*; and nine very short bursts in quick succession, called *teruah*. Each sound represents the remorse that Jews should feel for the mistakes they have made over the past year.

The sounding of the shofar is not just a sign of remorse. It is also a way for Jews to ask God to forgive them, if not for their own sakes, then for the sake of their ancestors. When the patriarch Abraham

This early-seventeenth-century painting portrays an angel preventing Abraham from offering his son Isaac as a sacrifice.

offered his son Isaac as a sacrifice to God, an angel stopped him just before he brought the knife down on his son. Searching for something else to sacrifice, he found a ram tangled by its horns in a nearby bush and offered it to God instead (Genesis 22). Even if Jews believe that they are not deserving of forgiveness, they ask God to forgive them for the sake of Abraham, who was willing to sacrifice his son to show his commitment to God.

Rosh Hashanah is also a time for celebration. The meals served then are similar to the Sabbath meals but with the addition of certain symbolic foods. For instance, the challah bread is dipped in honey, instead of being sprinkled with salt, in hope of a sweet year. Another custom is to dip slices of apple in honey and recite the words "May we have a year as sweet as apple in honey." Each community around the world has its own special foods and special wishes to recite to one another. For instance, some people eat pomegranates and say "May we have as many good deeds as there are seeds in a pomegranate." Sliced carrots, glazed in honey, eaten because they look a little like gold coins, are accompanied by the wish "May we have a wealthy year." Some people eat the head of a lamb or a fish and say "May we be as a head, and not as a tail." Beets are eaten with the statement "May our enemies run away from us," because the Hebrew word for beet is a pun on the word for "run away." Some families like to create new symbolic foods to pass down to the next generation and thus start new traditions.

Rosh Hashanah is the first of two holidays collectively known as the High Holidays. The second is Yom Kippur, the most solemn day in the Jewish calendar. Yom Kippur is a day of fasting and repentance. On this day, Jews believe, God determines the fate of each and every individual for the coming year. This is the last chance for people to show God how sincere they are in their attempts to overcome all the mistakes they have made.

People often dress in white and do not wear leather shoes or perfumes. Some rabbis have even compared Jews on Yom Kippur to angels who have risen above all bodily pleasures.

Most of the day of Yom Kippur is spent in the synagogue. The holiday begins in the evening with the *Kol Nidrei* service. The Holy Ark is opened, and all the Torah scrolls are removed. While most people consider *Kol Nidrei* a prayer, it is actually an enactment of a religious court, with the people holding the Torah scrolls acting as the judges. Following the cantor, the members of the congregation utter a formula asking the judges to absolve them of any oaths they may have made in the past year but failed to fulfill. Jews want to start the new year on a positive note, without any unfulfilled promises hanging over them.

An important part of the remainder of the service that night and the following day is called the *Vidui*, or Confession. This is a communal confession for a long list of sins, recited whether the person has committed them or not. The idea is that even if the individual has not committed one sin or another, there will likely be someone in the community who has. The community is responsible for all its members, even if it means confessing the sins of others and asking forgiveness on their behalf.

Yom Kippur reaches its climax just before sunset at the end of the day. The Holy Ark is opened, and the *Neilah* prayer is recited. *Neilah* (literally "the closing of the gates") is the last chance to plead with God for forgiveness before the day ends and the symbolic gates through which prayer reaches heaven are shut for the holiday. As the day ends, the shofar is blown and the entire congregation cries out the Shema as a final affirmation of its commitment to God. The Holy Ark is then shut, and everyone congratulates one another in the belief that God has heard them and their prayers will be answered. Jews then head home to break their fast and begin preparing for the next holiday, Sukkoth.

Sukkoth begins just five days after Yom Kippur, and there is much work to be done. It is the first of the Pilgrimage Festivals that, in the days when the Temple stood, Jews celebrated by traveling to Jerusalem to worship and offer sacrifices there. It is a harvest festival, and prayers for rain play an important role in the service and ritual. Since the prayers for winter rain are such an important part of this festival and since everyone—not only Jews—benefits from rain, sacrifices were once offered in the Temple for the prosperity of all the nations of the world. Sukkoth is the only holiday when Jews are explicitly commanded to be happy.

Sukkoth is also the one holiday not celebrated in the home. Instead, each family builds a little shack, called a sukkah, which they live in for the seven days of the holiday. Most people just eat in their sukkah, but some people sleep in it also.

From the outside, the sukkah looks like a few boards slapped together or a piece of canvas wrapped around some poles to make walls. Instead of a roof, branches or bamboo poles called *schach* are loosely thrown on top, so that it is still possible to see the stars twinkling between the gaps. The sukkah is only a temporary shelter, and the gaps in the roof remind Jews that real shelter comes only from God. Inside, the sukkah is richly decorated with posters and drawings. Fruits and vegetables are often hung from the roof and along the walls to remind people that this is the harvest season.

In ancient times, the harvest was the busiest time of the year. People worked from sunrise to sunset to get their crops in before the winter rains began. They often slept and ate in their fields, in little *sukkot (sukkot* is the plural of sukkah) so that they would not have to waste time going home and back during the day. As on many other holidays, Jews not only remember the way their ancestors lived, they reenact it too.

Many festivals are related to the main events that occurred during the Exodus, when the Jews left a life of slavery in Egypt to be a free nation in their own land. For forty years they wandered through the Sinai Desert, stopping at various waterholes until they reached the Promised Land. During that time, they probably lived in little huts similar to the sukkah, which they could put together easily and take apart as soon as they were ready to move on. By living in a sukkah, Jews are reenacting their ancestors' wanderings in the desert.

Another mitzvah unique to Sukkoth relates to the prayers said during the holiday. This is the only holiday that requires special "props" for the entire congregation as a part of the standard prayer service. During the service, Jews take branches from three trees—palm (*lulav*), myrtle (*hadas*), and willow (*aravah*)—and the fruit of a citron tree (*etrog*), which looks like a lemon, and wave them in six directions: front, back, right, left, up, and down. At another point in the service, they parade with them around the synagogue. This practice is the fulfillment of a commandment in the book of Leviticus (23:40), "And you shall take on the first day the fruit of goodly trees [the citron], branches of palm trees, and the boughs of leafy trees [myrtle], and willows of the brook, and you shall rejoice before the Lord your God seven days."

Rabbis and scholars have long struggled with this commandment, trying to understand what the various plants represent. One popular explanation compares them to different types of Jews. The citron has both a sweet smell and a sweet taste: it can be compared to someone who is both wise and does good deeds. The palm branch, which has a sweet taste but no smell, can be compared to someone who does good deeds but is not wise or learned. Similarly, the myrtle, which has a sweet smell but no edible fruit, can be compared to a wise person who performs no good deeds. Finally, the willow, which has no sweet smell and no sweet fruit, is like a person who is not learned and does good deeds. While all these people are different, it is only when they are

An Orthodox Jew carefully inspects a branch of myrtle that he will use during the holiday of Sukkoth.

brought together that the Jewish people are complete. It is impossible to leave anyone out.

Immediately after the week of Sukkoth is another short holiday called *Shemini Atzeret-Simchat Torah*. On this holiday, Jews make a final appeal to God for winter rains so that the next harvest will be fruitful. The holiday has also become a celebration of the completion of the reading of the Torah, which takes place in the synagogue every week over the course of the year. Everyone gathers in the synagogue to hear the final chapters of the book of Deuteronomy and also the first chapter of the book of Genesis, because every ending should also be a new beginning. During the service, all the Torah scrolls are removed from the Holy Ark and paraded around the synagogue seven times, with each member of the congregation taking turns marching with the Torah scrolls and even dancing with them. Until recently, only men danced with the Torah scrolls, but today most synagogues, even those that separate men and women, offer women an opportunity to carry the Torah scrolls and dance with them.

If Sukkoth is the major holiday of the fall season, then Pesach, or Passover, is the great holiday of spring. In fact, another name for the holiday is *Chag ha-Aviv*, the Festival of Spring. This is the season when the natural world comes back to life after a long winter. Trees bloom and flowers blossom; farmers see the first stalks of grain covering their fields with a rich carpet of green. In this season of birth and rebirth, Jews also celebrate their own birth as a religion and a people.

Passover commerorates the ancient Israelites' liberation from a life of slavery in Egypt with a series of rituals designed to act out that first night of freedom among family and friends. The most important of these rituals is the seder, a religious meal with special foods, customs, and songs, held on the first two nights of Passover.

The seder is special not only for the foods that Jews eat but also for the foods they do not eat. According to the Bible, the Israelites were in such a hurry to leave Egypt that they did not allow their bread to rise before they baked it. When they reached the desert and began to prepare their first meal as free men and women, all that they had for bread was thin, crisp crackers called matzo. Hence, Jews do not eat bread or any leavened products during Pesach (including cakes, cookies, beer, and other leavened products made of grain). Instead, they eat matzo, as their ancestors did in the desert. Eating matzo is an important part of the seder meal.

To remember the bitterness of slavery in Egypt, Jews also eat *maror* (bitter herbs) at the seder. To sweeten the herbs, they dip them in *charoset,* a paste made of apples, nuts, cinnamon, and wine, to remind them of the mortar that their ancestors used for making bricks in Egypt. The meal begins with a piece of green vegetable, such as parsley or scallion, to mark the coming of spring. This vegetable is dipped in salt water, in remembrance of the tears that the Jews' ancestors shed as slaves. All of these foods are arranged on a special seder plate, together with an egg, a symbol of birth, and a roasted bone with some meat on it, which represents the Passover sacrifice that was once offered in the Temple.

While eating these special foods, everyone reads from the Haggadah, a book that recounts the Exodus from Egypt through stories, legends, and songs. There are special parts written especially for young children, just to keep them interested in everything that is happening around them. The Haggadah opens with the *Ma Nishtana,* or Four Questions, and the youngest child asks why this night is different from every other night. The answers to these questions are the basis of the Haggadah. It ends with songs for the entire family, including *Chad Gadya,* about a little goat that is eaten by a cat that is bitten by a dog that is hit by a stick that is burned by a fire and continues in this way until God eventually slays the Angel of Death. Each time a new character or action is introduced, the song repeats

During the Passover seder, Jews celebrate with four cups of wine. A fifth cup is left untouched for the prophet Elijah, who according to tradition will one day usher in the final redemption of the Jewish people.

itself, with the children often acting out the sounds made by each of the characters as the story unfolds.

The middle days of Passover, like the middle days of Sukkoth, are called *Chol HaMoed*. During both holidays, special prayers are recited, and certain customs are kept. For instance, on *Chol HaMoed* of Sukkoth, Jews still eat in the sukkah, and on *Chol HaMoed* of Pesach, Jews eat matzo instead of bread. On the other hand, the days of *Chol HaMoed* are not celebrated like holidays, and Jews may go to work and do everything they would on a normal weekday. At Sukkoth, *Chol HaMoed* is followed by the holidays of *Shemini Atzeret* and *Simchat Torah*. At Passover, there are two more days of holiday, which are very similar to the Sabbath, except that Jews still eat matzo instead of bread.

In ancient times, people counted the days from Pesach until the next holiday, Shavuot, just seven weeks away. Seven weeks was the amount of time that Jews had to bring a sampling of their first fruits to the Temple in Jerusalem as an offering. Though Jews no longer bring offerings, they continue to count the days until Shavuot, the Festival of Weeks, a short holiday that marks the beginning of summer. This custom is called "counting the *Omer*," and the period between the two holidays is known as the *Omer*.

Shavuot, a two-day holiday, is probably the festival that is most connected to agriculture. At Shavuot, it is a tradition to read the book of Ruth because the story takes place during the grain harvest, and in many agricultural communities in Israel, people hold festive pageants and parades, during which they carry their crops throughout the village on richly decorated tractors and wagons.

Shavuot also has historical significance relating to the Exodus from Egypt. Shavuot occurs fifty days—seven weeks and a day—after the second day of Passover. According to an ancient tradition, after seven weeks of wandering in the desert, the Jews arrived at the foot of Mount Sinai to receive the Torah directly from God. According to the Bible (see Exodus 12:37), about 600,000 men between the ages of twenty and sixty—about two to three million people including women, children, and the elderly—stood at the foot of the mountain while God recited the Ten Commandments to Moses. God's revelation at Mount Sinai marked the transformation of the Israelites from a ragtag band of escaped slaves into a people and a religious community. According to the Bible, when Moses recited the commandments to the Israelites, the people all responded as one, "We will observe all that God has decreed; we will obey" (Exodus 24:7).

Though the Bible lists no special commandments for Shavuot apart from the one concerning special offerings of the first fruit in the Temple, many customs have developed around this holiday. For instance, since it marks the giving of the Torah, it is customary to stay up all night to study the Torah and review its commandments. As it is a summer holiday, it is customary to eat light dairy meals with cheesecake for dessert. To remember how God spoke directly to the Israelites at Mount Sinai, many synagogues recite a special poem called *Akdamut*: "If all the skies were parchment, and all the reeds were pens, and all the seas were ink. . . . It would still be impossible to describe the glory of God."

Hanukkah is one of several minor holidays celebrated to mark important historical events in Jewish history. Known as the Festival of Lights, Hanukkah occurs in mid-winter, at about the same time as Christmas. For eight nights, Jews light special lamps, or menorahs, in their windows. On the first night the central candle is lit to light one other. On the second night it lights two candles, and so on until all eight candles are lit on the last night. The candles are lit to remember a miracle that happened more than two thousand years ago.

During the time of the Second Temple, Jerusalem was occupied by the Seleucids, a Greek empire based in Syria. The Seleucid ruler

The Hanukkah candles are displayed in the windows of Jewish homes as a symbol of the struggle for religious freedom.

Antiochus IV Epiphanes was very hostile to the Jews and forbade them to practice their religion. In 167 B.C.E., after several years of hardship, one family, sometimes known as the Maccabees, led the people in a revolt against Antiochus and his armies. They fought many harsh battles and suffered many losses before the Jewish rebels led by Judah Maccabee liberated the Temple. After cleaning it out, they decided to light the menorah, a seven-branched candelabrum that stood in the center of the Temple building. The problem was that the Seleucids had desecrated all the oil, and they could find only enough pure oil to last one day, while it would take Judah and his followers eight days to prepare new oil. Still, Judah Maccabee insisted that they light the menorah and leave the rest to God.

The next day, when the Jews returned to the Temple, they found the lamps of the menorah still burning, as if they had just put oil in them. The lamps continued burning for eight days until new oil could be obtained. In honor of this miracle, Jews light their own menorahs for eight days, adding a candle each night to show how much greater the miracle was each day. The lighted menorah is placed in a window so that everyone passing by can see this reminder of the ancient miracle.

For Jews, Hanukkah is more than a reminder of an ancient miracle. It is a constant reminder that, like the Maccabees, each person has a responsibility to rise up against oppression and to struggle for basic human rights, including the freedom of religion. By adding lights to the menorah, Jews are stating their belief that even if one person stands up against oppression, that person will be joined by others until the whole world is filled with the light of freedom. As Rabbi Hillel wrote in the Talmud, "In a world where no one acts like a human being, try to take the initiative and be a human being" (Avot 2:5). This is also the lesson of Hanukkah.

Another historical holiday, Purim, occurs just one month before

The jewish calendar

It is impossible to give the exact dates on which Jewish holidays are celebrated because they follow a calendar different from the one we use in our day-to-day lives. The day does not begin at midnight but at sunset, which occurs at a slightly different time every day and even in different places on the same day. The Jewish Sabbath and Jewish holidays begin after the sun has already set.

The Jewish calendar is a lunar calendar, its months based on the cycle of the moon. There are twelve months (Tishrei, Cheshvan, Kislev, Tevet, Shevat, Adar, Nissan, Iyar, Sivan, Tammuz, Av, and Elul), each of which begins as soon as the first faint signs of new moon can be seen in the sky. In ancient times, a court called the Sanhedrin was convened to determine when each month would begin, and huge bonfires were lit on the mountaintops to signal the news to everyone. As the Jews became more dispersed, it became more difficult to spread the news to distant communities, and Jews began celebrating the holidays on different days.

To solve this problem, Hillel II, a descendant of Rabbi Hillel, devised a permanent calendar that could be used from year to year. His calendar limited the twelve lunar months to twenty-nine or thirty days so that each month corresponded as closely as possible to the phases of the moon. However, even before Hillel II, Jews realized that if they kept a purely lunar calendar, they would slowly fall behind the solar calendar of 365¼ days, and the holidays would fall in the wrong seasons. They solved this problem by adding a leap month, Adar II, every few years. Adar II is added seven times over nineteen years to ensure that the calendar keeps to the solar seasons and that Pesach, the holiday celebrating the birth of the Jewish people, always takes place in spring. Hillel incorporated the cycle of leap months into his calendar, which is still used by Jews today.

Passover. This holiday celebrates an event that took place about 475 B.C.E. (described in the book of Esther), when the Jews of the Persian empire were rescued from a plot to massacre them. According to the story, Haman, the grand vizier of the Persian king Ahasuerus, received royal consent to kill all the Jews in the country. What he did not know was that the queen, Esther, was secretly a Jew herself. After a series of events that led to the downfall of Haman, Esther tells the king of her Jewish identity and has the order revoked. Ahasuerus cancels his decree, Haman is punished, and Esther's uncle Mordecai, who plays a key role in the unfolding story, is appointed to replace him.

Since most of the events described in the book of Esther take place during parties, Purim is celebrated with parties and an enormous feast. There is a carnival atmosphere, and children and many adults dress up in costumes depicting the heroes (and villains) of the Purim story or even the latest action heroes. In the synagogue, the book of Esther is read to the community, and everyone joins in by booing, stamping their feet, and shaking noisemakers called *graggers* whenever Haman's name is mentioned. The morning before the feast everyone goes from house to house, delivering *mishloach manot* (gifts of food), to share the happiness with everyone else. They also make a point of giving *tzedakah*, or charity, to make sure that even the poorest people can participate in the celebration.

Costumes are part of the fun of Purim, but they also have a deeper significance. Esther was able to rescue the Jewish people because she disguised herself for many years in the Persian court and let the king know that she was Jewish only when it was absolutely necessary. Perhaps more important, the book of Esther is one of the rare books in the Bible where God is never mentioned. The climax occurs naturally, after a series of coincidences, and the story can easily be read like a nonreligious novel. This itself is an important message. God may not always be visible to people. He may sometimes be disguised by the

Costumes are an integral part of Purim, as these brightly dressed Israeli girls display.

natural world, but his influence can still be felt everywhere, even if people do not immediately realize it.

If Purim marks the happiest day in the Jewish year, Tishah-b'Ab marks the saddest. It was on this day that the Temple was destroyed, in both 586 B.C.E. and in 70 C.E. Coincidentally, many other tragic events in Jewish history occurred on Tishah-b'Ab. For example, in 1095, Pope Urban II declared the First Crusade, which led to the destruction of many Jewish communities across Europe; in 1290, King Edward of England signed an edict expelling the Jews from that country; and in 1914, World War I began on this day. It is a day of mourning and fasting, and in the synagogue the book of Lamentations is read while Jews sit on the floor listening as a sign of their humiliation.

A man and his son consult the Torah as part of their observance of Tishah-b'Ab. Jewish traditions are passed down by parents to their children.

Tishah-b'Ab has a happy twist to it. The Talmud claims that the messiah will be born on this day. In Jewish tradition, the messiah is a great Jewish leader who will usher in an age of peace and prosperity for all humanity. In other words, the Talmud seems to be saying that even when terrible events are happening in one place, a reason for hope is emerging somewhere else, even if people do not realize it. For instance, in 1492 King Ferdinand and Queen Isabella ordered the Jews to leave Spain by Tishah-b'Ab. According to the legend, Columbus set sail for the New World on that same day. While he and his sailors likely saw the Jews boarding the boats to take them away, Columbus himself was setting off to discover new lands in North America that would one day become the most vibrant center of Jewish life. Tishah-b'Ab in 1492 was a time of mourning for the Jews of Spain, while, unknown to them, new opportunities were opening up for their descendants beyond the horizon.

five

LIFE CYCLES

question: what is the technical term for a jewish child over eight days old, who has not been circumcised?

Answer: A girl.

This may be one of the oldest Jewish jokes around, but like many jokes, it offers a peek into the world of its subject matter, in this case, the Jewish people. For most Jews, it is inconceivable that a newborn male child would not be circumcised and entered into the covenant of Abraham—a promise God made to the patriarch Abraham that he will make Abraham the forefather of many great nations (see Genesis 17:1–16).

Circumcision, that is, the surgical removal of the foreskin, is one of the oldest commandments in the Bible—when Abraham was already ninety-nine years old, he was commanded by God to circumcise himself and all the males in his household (see Genesis 17:11). This sign, a physical expression of God's promise to Abraham, has been maintained by his descendants, Jews (through his son Isaac) and Arabs (through his son Ishmael) alike, up until today. For a Jewish infant boy, it is the first of many rituals that will mark him as a member of the Jewish people.

In North America today, it is common for non-Jews to be circumcised too. Until recently, however, circumcision could be used as evidence that someone was Jewish. In Europe it was rare for anyone but Jews to be circumcised, and in times of persecution, male Jews could be identified by having them pull down their pants.

For male Jews, however, their circumcision, or *brit* (sometimes also *bris*; literally, "covenant") is a sign of great pride. Even in times of persecution, it reminded them of the promise that God made to Abraham that his descendants will one day be a great nation, dedicated to the ideal of *tikkun olam*, or repairing the world. Circumcision is a sign of this commitment to *tikkun olam*. It represents the belief that while God created each and every human being, he left people with the responsibility of completing the act of creation, in this case by removing the unnecessary foreskin.

The *brit* is usually conducted on the eighth day after the baby boy is born. If, however, the baby is premature or unhealthy for any reason, it may be postponed until a doctor determines that the child is ready. In the past, the *brit* was performed by a *mohel*, a person with special training in both the religious and the medical aspects of circumcision. In modern times, the *mohel* is often someone with medical training as well.

The entire community is invited to the *brit*, so that everyone can celebrate as a new member enters the community. The child is placed on a pillow and passed to the various friends and relatives who will serve as godparents to him. He is then placed on his father's lap, and the *mohel* places a tiny drop of wine on the baby's lips to reduce the pain. The diaper is removed, and the *mohel* recites a prayer and then quickly performs the operation. It is over in an instant, and as soon as the baby cries out, all the guests shout *mazal tov* (congratulations) and wish the infant a life devoted to Torah, family, and good deeds.

As a child grows older, he or she is gradually trained to perform various commandments and to recite simple prayers, such as the Shema. Educating children is one of the most important commandments in the Torah and is considered to be the responsibility of the parents no less than that of the teacher. In the past, many customs developed to celebrate milestones in the child's life. The Bible suggests that there was once a ceremony when a child stopped breast-feeding (see Genesis 21:8), and

A man shields his face with his Passover prayer book.

many Orthodox communities today still celebrate a boy's first haircut at the age of three.

In many Orthodox communities, the first day of school is also a big event for Jewish children. Until recently, parents wrapped their children in a tallith and walked them to school. Upon arrival, the teacher presented each child with his first book, usually a siddur, or prayer book, with the letters of the first page covered with honey. Parents and teachers encouraged the new students to lick the letters in the hope that they would always associate reading and learning with something sweet. While few Orthodox communities still follow this exact custom, in many Jewish schools teachers hand out sweets on the first day of school for the same reason.

As children approach puberty, they begin studying for another great event in their life, a bar mitzvah for boys and a bat mitzvah for girls. In the United States, this ceremony is often the highlight of a young Jewish person's growth. It is the first time that young Jews are called to the Torah in the synagogue to chant from the Torah scrolls. It is hard to imagine that the bar mitzvah celebration is only a few hundred years old and the bat mitzvah ceremony began much later, in the early twentieth century.

Nevertheless, puberty has always been an important milestone in a young Jew's life. In the past, it signaled a time when young people could leave school and go to work or get married and have children of their own. Few Jewish families had the resources to enable their children to continue in school as teens. Among poorer Jews, everyone was expected to pitch in to support the family. By the time they were teens, young people were regarded as full adults by the community with the same responsibilities.

In the past, puberty also marked the time when young Jews were expected to begin performing the commandments kept by adults. They were considered responsible for their own actions, and if they did anything wrong, it was they and not their parents who faced the consequences. Since they were now full members of the community, boys were honored by being called up to the Torah in the synagogue to recite the blessings for the community and chant from the weekly reading. After the reading, the parents recited a special blessing thanking God for relieving them of their responsibility for the child, who was now expected to make his own way in the world. After services, friends and family gathered for a modest toast in honor of the young member, who would now participate fully in the community.

In the modern-day world, parents continue to be responsible for their children long after their bar or bat mitzvah. Like many old ceremonies, the bar and bat mitzvah have assumed new meaning for young Jews—as an opportunity to declare their identification with the Jewish community and its values. After their bar or bat mitzvah, Jews are considered full members of the community and can be called to the Torah and to participate in all parts of the service in the synagogue. They have studied for this day, but even after the ceremony is over, their studies and participation in the community should continue. In many Reform and Conservative synagogues, a new ceremony, Confirmation, has been introduced when the boy or girl is an older teen. Confirmation classes offer teenagers a chance to continue their Jewish studies in greater depth, to participate more actively in Jewish rituals, and to gain experience in performing the mitzvoth.

Beginning in the 1980s, a new component, the *tzedakah* project, has been added to many of the programs in which Jewish teens prepare for their bar or bat mitzvah. *Tzedakah*, meaning acts of charity and kindness, are among the most important mitzvoth that Jews can perform, as individuals and as a community. To train children in *tzedakah*, they are each asked to think of ways to transform their bar or bat mitzvah celebration into an event that celebrates giving to others. Invitations might include requests to bring used books or magazines, cans of food, or other items to the party so they can later be distributed by the family to the needy. In congregations everywhere, young bar mitzvah boys and bat mitzvah girls have found special ways to share the joy of their celebration with others through exciting *tzedakah* projects that reflect their interests, concerns, and dreams.

As they grow older, young Jews begin to plan their own lives and many consider creating their own families. Until about one hundred years ago, most of these decisions were made for them by their parents, who employed a *shadchan*, or matchmaker, to find the perfect bride or groom for their child. Anyone who has seen the musical *Fiddler on the Roof* remembers Yente the Matchmaker, a busybody who pairs off couples for a fee—and usually fails miserably at it. *Fiddler on the Roof* is based on a series of Yiddish stories written by Sholom Aleichem more than a century ago. At the time he wrote those stories, the matchmaker was the butt of jokes among young people who wanted to fall in love and find their own marriage partners.

Only some Orthodox Jews still rely on the services of a matchmaker to find a spouse for themselves or their children. Almost all young Jews now marry a partner of their own choosing.

Jewish wedding celebrations can be lengthy events with parties before and after the ceremony lasting as long as two weeks. On the Saturday before the wedding, the bride and groom may invite their friends to special parties held in their homes. The groom, and in some congregations the bride, is given special honors in the synagogue and is called to read the *maftir*, the last portion of the Torah read that week. When the reading is over, the congregation showers him with candies so that he may have a sweet life.

In North African and Middle Eastern countries, these parties may extend until the day of the wedding. Traditionally, the palms of the bride's hands are dyed with red henna as a sign of good luck.

A bride and groom share a tallith as they stand before the rabbi on their wedding day.

Most Jewish wedding ceremonies take place in the late afternoon or evening. The day leading to the ceremony is a solemn occasion. Many Jews fast, and there is a custom for the bride and groom not to see or even speak to each other until just before the ceremony. (Some couples will not see each other for as long as a month before the wedding.) In Orthodox communities, both the bride and the groom are escorted by their closest friends to immerse themselves in the *mikvah*, or ritual bath, on the day of the wedding. They come out of the water reborn and ready to start a new life together.

A traditional wedding begins with separate parties for the bride and the groom, held in different rooms. The highlight of the groom's party is the signing of an engagement agreement, based on an ancient tradition when weddings were negotiated between families. Once the agreement is signed, the mothers of the bride and groom smash a plate as another symbol of good luck for the young couple.

In ancient times, when women were veiled, it was easy for the family of a bride to fool the groom by marrying him off to another daughter, rather than the one he selected. Such a story is mentioned in the Bible: Laban gave Jacob his elder daughter Leah, even though he was in love with her younger sister, Rachel (see Genesis 29:15–30). To remember this incident, the friends of the groom dance him to the bridal party. Shortly before they arrive, a veil is placed over the bride's face. When he reaches the bride, the groom lifts the veil to ensure that this is the woman he wants to marry, and the ceremony continues.

For the wedding ceremony, the bride and groom stand under a canopy, called a *chuppah*, which is supported on four poles. The canopy represents the roof of the new home that the young couple will build. It has no walls, because even as they build a home for themselves, the husband and wife must always look out for the needs of others. Their home should be modeled on the tent of Abraham, which, according to legend, was kept open in all directions so that he could always see if others were in need. Traditionally, the groom enters the *chuppah* first, followed by the bride. In Orthodox and Conservative weddings, the bride circles the groom seven times, symbolically building the walls of their new home. It is also the bride's turn to see if the groom is really the man she has chosen to marry.

It is customary that no jewelry be worn under the *chuppah*. Both the bride and the groom are marrying each other out of love, not because of any material wealth that one or the other might have.

Once the bride and groom are standing side by side, a rabbi recites the marriage blessing, called *kiddushin* (literally, "sanctification"), and the couple shares a glass of wine. The groom then recites, "Behold you are consecrated to me according to the law of Moses and Israel," and places a simple gold band on the bride's forefinger. In many congregations, it is common for the bride to reciprocate by reciting the same formula and placing a ring of her own on the groom's finger. The couple is then officially married according to Jewish law.

The ceremony, however, is not yet over. The *ketubah*, or marriage agreement, is read out loud. In this agreement, often an elaborately decorated document, the groom states that he will provide for the bride financially, and he describes the clothing and jewelry he will buy her and the arrangements he will make for her in case of divorce. Although the wedding is a happy occasion, there are also many practical details to attend to. Many young Jews have opted to rewrite the *ketubah* to reflect a more egalitarian approach to marriage and the love that the couple shares.

Rabbis, family members, and other honored guests are then invited to join the couple under the *chuppah* to recite seven blessings calling on God to keep the couple happy. After the blessings the bride and groom sip more wine and begin their life together.

Before they leave the *chuppah*, the bride and groom perform one more act to complete the wedding. They place a glass on the floor and stomp on it. In Jewish tradition, even in times of happiness the suffering of others, whether in the past or the present, must not be forgotten. As long as there are people anywhere in need, by breaking the glass, the couple is reminded that they cannot be perfectly happy themselves. Today, some couples choose to stomp on a lightbulb instead of a glass, since it shatters more easily.

Once the glass is shattered, everyone shouts *mazal tov,* and the couple is escorted to a small room where they can spend a few minutes alone together, relaxing from a strenuous day, before rejoining their guests for the party. Even after the wedding is over, many Orthodox and Conservative couples still have a busy week ahead of them, with six more nights of parties, given by family and friends in their honor. At each party, the seven blessings recited under the *chuppah* are repeated by the guests as a prayer for the couple's future happiness together.

Traditionally, Jewish funerals are simple affairs, and the dead are treated with great dignity. One of the greatest honors in the community is to prepare the body of the deceased for burial.

In Jewish tradition, a body is never left untended from the moment of death until the burial. The rabbis of the Talmud described elaborate burial ceremonies that once occured but complained that more money was being spent on the dead than on the living. In response, they decreed that a very simple ceremony should take place to preserve the dignity of the deceased without being a burden to the family.

Traditional Jews allow no makeup or jewelry on the corpse. The body is washed and wrapped in a simple white shroud, often with a tallith over it, and then placed in a plain wooden coffin containing no metal—wooden pegs hold the boards together. In keeping with God's words to Adam, no attempt is made to preserve the body, "For dust you are, and to dust you shall return." Once the body is ready and the casket is sealed, *shomrim* (guards) sit with it at the funeral

A group of girls helps a friend light candles at her bat mitzvah celebration. A new Jewish custom has friends and family light thirteen candles in honor of bar mitzvah boys and bat mitzvah girls.

parlor around the clock, reciting from the book of Psalms until the funeral is held. While many Jews no longer keep these customs, the basic principle of maintaining the dignity of the deceased with simple preparations and a simple service is kept by all Jews.

The funeral is as much a time for the family of the deceased to express its grief as it is a time to honor the deceased. Before the service begins, friends of the family members help them rip their shirts as a sign of mourning. Rabbis, friends, and family are invited to deliver brief eulogies for the departed, and a prayer for the dead is recited.

Jewish tradition describes caring for the dead as a *chesed shel emet*, a genuine act of kindness, since people cannot expect the dead to pay them back. For this reason, once the coffin is lowered into the grave, everyone helps to shovel dirt over it. It is customary to toss the

women in judaism

Rituals, with all their significance, are the basis of Jewish life. It is, therefore, ironic that until recently so many of the rituals seemed to neglect women. Until the twentieth century, traditional Judaism did not require women to perform positive commandments that were linked to a specific time. They were not required to pray at set times or to put on tefillin in the morning. They were not expected to eat in a sukkah during Sukkoth or to hear the shofar blown on Rosh Hashanah. While many women who were able made every effort to perform some of these commandments, they were not obligated to do so. Many of the prominent rituals were observed only by men.

That is not to say that there were no mitzvoth that women were expected to keep. They were required to observe those commandments that prohibited various acts, such as working on Shabbat or eating on Yom Kippur. Certain commandments, such as teaching young children, have been the responsibility of Jewish women for centuries, and the lighting of candles to mark the beginning of Shabbat has been almost exclusively the domain of women, even though it is a positive commandment linked to a specific time and even though many men now light the candles as well. And of course women were obligated to perform all the same acts of charity and kindness as men.

In public life though, women, with few exceptions, were generally excluded. Religious law forbade them from serving as witnesses in court or as judges. Social customs common among all cultures at the time prevented them from receiving public honors in the synagogue, such as being called to read from the Torah.

One comforting thought is that Judaism provides many examples of how the religion has evolved to adapt to changing conditions in the world. At one time, the Temple was the center of Jewish worship; today it is the synagogue. Similarly, while women were once excluded from many aspects of Jewish life, the Reform and Conservative movements of today have granted full equality to women, and Orthodox women have taken responsibility for performing many of the mitzvoth that were once the domain of men. Since the early 1970s, the Reform movement has ordained women as rabbis. The Conservative movement followed a few years later, and today the Orthodox movement is seeking innovative ways to include women in public life as teachers and community leaders.

Change may be slow, but each segment of the Jewish community is addressing the issues concerning women in its own way. Today practically every young Jewish girl in the United States celebrates a bat mitzvah; yet the first girl to mark the occasion, Judith Kaplan, did so only in 1922. While no one questions the idea that Jewish girls should get an education, it is hard to imagine that the first school specifically for Orthodox girls was opened by Sarah Schenirer in Krakow, Poland, in 1917.

Today, Reform, Conservative, Reconstructionist, and Orthodox Jews may debate the pace at which change is taking place, but no one can deny that change is occurring, and women have already assumed leadership positions in their communities as rabbis, cantors, and teachers. This trend can be expected to continue.

first few scoops of earth holding the shovel backward, to show how reluctant everyone is to part with the deceased. When the grave has been filled, the members of the immediate family remove their shoes, another sign of mourning, and walk between two columns of friends and family, who recite the traditional formula "May God comfort you among the mourners of Zion and Jerusalem."

For the next seven days, the family will remain at home, sitting on low stools to represent their sense of loss. All the mirrors in the house are covered: one cannot be vain at such a time of grief. There is a custom for family members to remove their shoes and avoid perfumes, further signs of mourning. For the next week, friends and relatives will drop by for visits and bring them all their meals. Traditionally, they encourage the family to talk about the deceased and revisit fond memories. As the guests leave, they often recite "May God comfort you among the mourners of Zion and Jerusalem." This week-long period is called the *shivah*, the Hebrew word for "seven."

For the children of the deceased, the mourning period lasts for the next year. Many Jews do not attend parties during this period, nor do they accept any special honors in the synagogue; although they attend synagogue regularly to recite the kaddish, a prayer that praises God. It makes no mention of the deceased, but for Jews it is a way of accepting God's judgment, even if those who have suffered a loss cannot understand it. As the Bible teaches in the book of Ecclesiastes, life is full of contradictions: "A time for tears, a time for laughter, a time for mourning, a time for dancing" (Ecclesiastes 3:4). In Judaism, this is what the life cycle is all about.

six

BASIC BELIEFS

While the saying "Actions speak louder than words" does not appear in the Bible or Talmud, it sums up the basic Jewish approach to belief: People are judged not on what they say but on what they do. All human beings, no matter what their religion, can be righteous and good, as long as they are kind to others and keep basic moral precepts. Each and every human being can be a *tzaddik*, a righteous person, and there are many righteous people, whether or not they are recognized as such.

What distinguishes Jews from followers of any other religion? There are the 613 commandments that only Jews are required to follow. There is the sense of kinship that comes from sharing a common history and culture, as well as a language, customs, and beliefs.

The rabbis of the Middle Ages debated exactly what it is that Jews are required to believe. Some made lists of the tenets they felt were essential to the Jewish religion. Other rabbis, challenging these lists, added beliefs and removed others. The most famous list and the one most widely accepted was composed by Maimonides, a Jewish sage who lived in Egypt in the latter half of the twelfth century. He called his list the Thirteen Principles of Faith. Some rabbis, quoting other works by Maimonides, questioned whether he actually believed all thirteen of his statements. It is likely that he did. Maimonides was careful to make his list deliberately vague so as to encompass many different shades of meaning.

Each statement of Maimonides's list begins with the phrase, "I believe with a complete belief." His list runs as follows:

1. **God exists.**

2. **There is only one God who cannot be divided.**

3. **God is a spiritual being, without any physical body.**

4. **God has no beginning and no end. He exists for all eternity.**

5. **Only God, and none of his creations, may be worshipped.**

6. **God revealed himself to humanity through a series of prophets.**

7. **Moses was the greatest of these prophets.**

8. **God gave his law, the Torah, to the Israelite ancestors of the Jewish people as they were gathered around Mount Sinai.**

9. **The Torah that God gave the Israelites cannot be changed.**

10. **God knows the future and is aware of what every individual will do.**

11. **Evil will be punished, and good will be rewarded.**

12. **One day a messiah will come to redeem the Jewish people and the entire world.**

13. **One day the dead will be resurrected.**

While many of these beliefs are shared by other religions, such as Christianity and Islam, some are distinctly Jewish and may well be a response to the beliefs of these other religions. For instance, the second belief, that there is only one God who cannot be divided, may be a response to the Christian belief in the Trinity. Similarly, the statement that Moses was the greatest of the prophets, which rarely appears in the lists of any other rabbis, may be a response to the Muslim belief that Muhammad was the greatest prophet. A careful examination of the list can bring a better understanding of what Jews believe today.

The idea that God exists seems to be a given in any Western religion. It is interesting to note that nowhere does Maimonides define what God is. There is considerable room for Jews to form their own definition of God or even to question whether a concept such as God can be defined at all. Some Jews define God as a spiritual being who created the universe and rules over it in every detail. Other Jews define God as the spirit of fellowship that exists between human beings or between human beings and the world around them. Each of these interpretations falls within the basic tenets of Judaism as enumerated by Maimonides.

The next three beliefs describe what God is not. He is one, as Jews recite in the Shema, and cannot be divided. He has no earthly body, and thus, all the descriptions of God in the Bible are metaphors for his actions. When Moses reminds the Israelites that God brought them out of Egypt with a "mighty hand and an outstretched arm" (Deuteronomy 26:8), he was using a common expression. He did not mean that God actually has a hand or an arm. According to some scholars, Maimonides intended this principle of faith to be a rejection of idolatry, in which God is given physical attributes, such as in the form of a statue. It may also be a rejection of the divinity of Jesus Christ, who is believed by Christians to be God in human form. In this sense, the idea that God has no earthly form is similar to the idea that God cannot be divided. Nor does God have any beginning or end. God always was and always will be, regardless of whether human beings recognize this or not.

Throughout history, people have claimed to be doing what God wants, even while they committed the most horrific crimes against other human beings. Countless wars have been fought over religion, and even today, people claim to be doing God's will when they are killing others. Maimonides responds to these people who claim to be fulfilling God's wishes by describing how God communicated with human beings through a series of prophets, whose words are recorded in the Bible. The prophet Isaiah, for example, described an era of peace where "the wolf lives with the lamb, the panther lies down with the kid, calf and lion cub feed together with a little boy to lead them" (Isaiah 11:6). The prophets may have scolded the Israelites and other nations for their sins, but they also offered a message of hope and a firm belief in a better world for everyone.

Moses was the greatest of the prophets because he gave the Jewish people the Torah, the source of all the commandments. All the prophets that follow Moses simply repeat the basic beliefs that appear in the first five books of the Bible and describe the outcome of following—or failing to follow—the commandments.

In his book, *Sefer ha-Kuzari,* another medieval Jewish philosopher, Rabbi Judah Halevi, described an imaginary conversation between a rabbi and the king of the Khazars, a people that lived in central Asia who converted to Judaism sometime in the late eighth or early ninth century. According to the story, the king wanted to know what the true faith was, and so he brought religion scholars from around the world to his court, including a Christian, a Muslim, and a Jew. When the Jew, who spoke last, was asked to prove the truth of his religion, he described how God gave the Torah to the Israelites on Mount Sinai and recited the Ten Commandments before millions of witnesses. Rabbi Judah Halevi wrote that the Jew's words eventually persuaded the king to adopt Judaism as his religion.

While the story is likely fictional, it expresses a basic part of traditional Jewish belief. God revealed himself not only to the prophets but also to an entire people when he gave the Torah to Moses. Today many Jews question the historical accuracy of the biblical account, but they still adhere, in one way or another, to the idea that the Torah is a special book in which God makes his will known. Even if some Jews reject many of the commandments as outdated or irrelevant to the modern world, they still find the overall message of the Torah—to be compassionate and to act kindly—as important today as it was to their ancestors three thousand years ago. It remains for today's Jews to find ways to interpret the Torah and make its message significant in their own lives. A common saying that reflects this belief is that all Jews, no matter when they live, stand in spirit at Mount Sinai to receive the Torah.

According to Maimonides, the Torah cannot be changed. One of the great questions of the modern era is whether values and morals are relative or not. Is it acceptable to kill or steal if an entire society believes that it is? A story in the Talmud tells that the Israelites were not God's first choice when he decided to give the Torah to the world. The legend describes how God went from nation to nation, asking if any would accept the Torah. Each nation refused, claiming that the commandments were contrary to its people's way of life. Only the Israelites answered, "We will observe all that God has decreed; we will obey" (Exodus 24:7). They accepted the idea that there was an absolute morality contained in the Torah, even if the precise details of that morality can be discussed and debated. According to Jews, it is this moral code described in the Torah that can never be changed.

The belief that God knows the future and all that people will do is difficult to understand. If God is omniscient and he knows what someone will do, how can people be blamed for their wrongdoings? After all, if God knows how a person will act, then those actions have already been determined, and there is no way for the person to behave otherwise. This belief runs counter to another basic belief, that everyone has the freedom to choose whether to do good or evil (though Maimonides does not include that belief in his Thirteen Principles).

While many religions, including most forms of Islam, believe in predetermination (the belief that all actions are determined before they occur), many rabbis have struggled with the idea and devised compromises to resolve the apparent paradox. They did not want to suggest a limit to God's knowledge, but at the same time, they wanted each human being to have freedom of choice. Among the many solutions they devised is that God knows all the options available to an individual, but each person has the freedom to choose them.

Another difficult principle to understand, one that is common to almost all lists of beliefs, is the idea that evil will be punished and good will be rewarded. The entire book of Job in the Bible addresses this very question, as does the first chapter of the Talmud. "Is this really true," the rabbis ask, "when all around us we see good people suffering while bad people thrive?" After thousands of years, the question is still being discussed, most recently in a popular book by Rabbi Harold S. Kushner, *When Bad Things Happen to Good People.*

One simple answer is that good people will be rewarded and bad people punished in the afterlife. While many religions claim this, the rabbis were hesitant to accept such a neat answer. There is no direct mention of the afterlife anywhere in the Bible, and very little about it can be found in any of the writings of the rabbis. That is not to say that Jews do not believe in an afterlife. Many do, but even they claim that it is so remote and so unknowable that it is impossible to comprehend. According to all Jews, the primary goal of humanity should be to transform this world into an earthly paradise rather than to work for the reward of a paradise after death.

The Talmud avoids giving a definitive answer on this matter, preferring instead to explain an incident described in the Bible. After receiving the Ten Commandments, Moses begged God, "Show me your glory" (Exodus 33:18), to which God answered, "You cannot see my face . . . for man cannot see me and live" (Exodus 33:20). Since God has no face (the third principle), Moses's question must be interpreted as a metaphor. According to the rabbis of the Talmud,

Moses really asked God, "How is it that the righteous man suffers while the wicked man thrives," to which God answered, "No living being can understand my ways." About 150 years ago, a Danish philosopher named Søren Kierkegaard argued that in religion it is necessary to make a "leap of faith" and accept certain ideas that extend beyond one's common sense. For many Jews, the belief that evil will eventually be punished and good rewarded is precisely that leap of faith. For others, it is enough to believe in an afterlife where people will receive their just desserts.

The final two beliefs refer to events that have not yet taken place and that Maimonides himself claimed are open to interpretation. For thousands of years, Jews have been waiting for a messiah to come and lead them out of exile and back to the promised land of Israel, where they will live in peace. For some Jews the Messiah is a specific individual, a direct descendant of King David who will reveal himself, possibly through a series of miracles, and bring about this new era of independence for the Jewish people. For other Jews the Messiah is a metaphor for a future era when all of humanity learns to overcome its differences and live in peace. According to both groups, the way to bring the Messiah is to perform the commandments and act kindly to one another. In one text, Maimonides writes that if a person leads the Jewish people to freedom, rebuilds the Temple as a place of worship for all nations, and begins to resolve the problems facing the world, then it can be safely assumed that this individual is the Messiah. Perhaps he was hinting that the potential to bring the era of the Messiah lies in each person.

The last principle described by Maimonides, the resurrection of the dead at some future time, is the most enigmatic. Maimonides himself writes that no one really understands what it means to be resurrected. Is it the physical resurrection of all people who ever lived? Will people live normal lives? Will they be faced with death again? Will they be resurrected as adults or as children? All that Maimonides says is that this day will happen long after the coming of the Messiah. The resurrection of the dead is yet another stage in human development, one that all people should strive for, even if the details are uncertain.

In some way, the idea that better times lie ahead is also a warning. Many devout Jews believe that the Messiah might appear at any moment. They anticipate his coming with every breath. One rabbi, a century ago, kept a packed suitcase beside his bed so that when the Messiah came, he could immediately follow him.

What Maimonides seems to be saying is that Jews must not be complacent. There is no such thing as a perfect world. There will always be ways to make the world better for ourselves and for others. The Messianic era is something to struggle for and look forward to, but even then, as the Talmud teaches, "The day is short, and the task is great . . . and it is not up to you to complete the task" (Avot 2:15–16). There is always so much more to do.

is god a He?

When speaking of God, it is necessary to choose a pronoun to go along with the name. In most religions, the pronoun is he. Does this imply that God is a male? How could he be if he has no physical form or attributes?

This is just one example of how inadequate language is when talking about God. People are limited in the way they understand God by how they perceive the world around them, and in English-speaking societies, this means dividing the beings with which they interact, including God, into either he's or she's. It would seem disrespectful to describe God as a big It.

This problem does not exist in every language. Some languages, such as Japanese and Hungarian, make no distinction between he and she, and so everyone, including God, is an it. In a language such as Hebrew, however, the original language of the Bible, every single object, including tables and vegetables, is assigned a random gender—in Hebrew, tables are masculine, and lamps are feminine.

In Jewish sources, many different names are ascribed to God. In the Bible, two of the most popular names are יהוה (literally, Yahweh, though it is always pronounced Adonai) and אלוהים (pronounced Elohim). There are also many other names, including *El*, *Shaddai*, *Tzur* (literally, "rock") and Shalom ("peace"). Many rabbinical texts refer to the presence of God as the Shechinah, which is a feminine noun. Two thousand years ago, Jewish mystics described specific characteristics of God associated with each name. They explained that some of these are "male attributes" while others are "female attributes." It is only human limitations that define God as one at the expense of the other.

seven

WHAT NEXT?

when the first Temple was destroyed, in 586 B.C.E., it seemed as if the end had finally come for the Jewish people. As the Jews were marched off from Jerusalem into exile, many of them never to see their homes again, according to legend Abraham rose from his grave to speak to God. "You promised me that my children would be as numerous as the sand along the seashore and the stars in the heavens. How could you possibly do this to my children?"

God frowned in response and said, "This time they have gone too far, and now they must be punished."

Abraham turned back, but his son Isaac rose from his grave and begged God to act mercifully toward the Jewish people. He was followed by Jacob, Moses, and King David. Each rose from his grave to beg forgiveness for the Jewish people, but God refused to listen to them.

Finally, as the Jews passed the small town of Bethlehem, Rachel, the wife of Jacob, rose from her tomb to cry for her children. When God looked down and saw her, he relented, because even God cannot bear to witness the tears of a mother mourning for her children. He bent down and said: "Stop your weeping, dry your eyes, your hardships shall be redressed. . . . There is hope for your descendants" (Jeremiah 31:16–17).

The promise of hope for the future has kept the Jewish people going, even in the darkest hours. In 70 C.E., more than six hundred years after the Jews were first led into exile, the Romans were poised to destroy the Second Temple. The belief that there was always hope for the future may have inspired Rabbi Yochanan Ben Zakkai, one of the leading sages of that period, to appear before the Roman emperor Vespasian and appeal to him to spare the town of Yavneh and its sages. Even if the Temple was lost, there would still be hope if some Jews, somewhere, would be allowed to study the Torah and keep the commandments. Though the Temple was destroyed, the emperor granted the rabbi his wish, and the Jewish people survived to rebuild their religious life around the synagogue and the study of the Torah.

More than half a century ago, it was this ancient promise of a better future that may have inspired Jews to resist the Nazis during the Holocaust. Some, such as Mordecai Anielewicz, took up arms and fought their oppressors, while others, such as Anne Frank, hid accounts of what they witnessed for future generations to find. Anielewicz and Anne Frank could not have known that the Jews would have an independent state of their own and that a Jewish community would flourish in the United States, but as Anne Frank wrote in her diary, "God never deserted our people. Right through the ages there were Jews. Through the ages they suffered, but it also made us strong."

The Jews of the United States are very fortunate. They face fewer problems of racism and anti-Semitism than their ancestors faced for centuries. They are a relatively affluent community that has succeeded in realizing the American dream. Jewish schools and academic institutions are flourishing. Second- and third-generation Jewish Americans are well integrated into all parts of American life, and an observant Jew, Joe Lieberman, even ran for the office of vice president of the United States in 2000 and entered the race as a presidential candidate in 2004.

With success, however, come new challenges that must be faced if Judaism is to survive in the United States. Although the United States

A pious Jew kisses the stones of the Western Wall, the last remnant of the Second Temple and Judaism's holiest site.

has the largest Jewish population in the world, many people born to Jewish families know little about their religion and history. Some have begun to assimilate into American life at the expense of their Jewish identity.

Jews have always learned from the cultures that surrounded them and adopted those ideas that would enrich their own religion. By becoming part of the American experience, Jews have assimilated values such as democracy and equality for women into their own belief system.

Still, there are fewer Jews who continue to celebrate their religion in the synagogue and with their families. For some Jews, basic rituals like the bar and bat mitzvah have become little more than an excuse to host a big party. As Jews enter the twenty-first century, they are challenged to find new ways to ensure that their religion continues to be meaningful in a modern world.

Many individuals and organizations have responded to the challenge. Young Jews are starting to re-examine the Bible, Talmud, and other Jewish texts to find messages that resonate with them. Many of them are involved in groups devoted to *tikkun olam* through special programs to promote social justice, the environment, and other key issues. Others are investigating Jewish music, books, and film to reinvigorate Jewish culture. Some Jews take an especial interest in the State of Israel or in the well-being of Jews in those countries where they face excessive discrimination or do not share the same rights granted to Americans. Some Jews are reinventing religious services by creating new rituals that reflect modern concerns. One example is the Freedom Seder, which was begun by Jews involved in the American civil rights movement in the 1960s. The readings combine traditional Jewish texts with works by modern civil rights activists to inspire the participants to play an active role in *tikkun olam*. Other Jews adhere as much as possible to the ancient laws and customs while finding ways to apply them in a rapidly changing world. They are investigating the texts to find out what Judaism has to say about contemporary issues such as abortion, stem-cell research, and the ethics of war.

There is no one answer as to what will keep the Jewish people alive and thriving over the next century. There is, however, an ancient promise made to Rachel more than two and a half millennia ago: "There is hope for your descendants."

When the Israeli astronaut Ilan Ramon flew into space aboard the space shuttle *Challenger*, he brought two items with him to represent his Jewish heritage. One was a small Torah, the other a drawing of the Earth as seen from the Moon, made by a young boy, Petr Ginz, in the Terezín concentration camp, shortly before he was sent to the gas chamber in Auschwitz.

Petr Ginz spent the last years of his life under the worst imaginable conditions. Nevertheless, as can be seen from his writing and his artwork, he seems to have believed that the world is still a beautiful place, if only it was viewed from the right perspective—in his case, the moon. What Ilan Ramon may not have realized was that by taking this picture and a copy of the Torah into space, he was representing a core message of Judaism. The world really can be a beautiful place. All that people need to make it so is a guidebook, the Torah, and hope.

TIME LINE

3758 B.C.E.
The date traditionally given for the creation of the world.

about 2000
Abraham, the first Patriarch, comes to the belief that there is only one
God. He leaves his home in Mesopotamia, now Iraq, and travels to
the Land of Canaan, now Israel, where God promises him that he will
be the father of great nations. He has two sons: Isaac, the traditional
ancestor of the Jewish people, and Ishmael, the traditional ancestor of
the Arab people.

about 1700
Jacob, the grandson of Abraham, settles in Egypt, where one of his
sons, Joseph, is adviser to the pharaoh. The small clan grows into a
sizable minority, which is persecuted and enslaved by the Egyptians.

about 1250
Led by Moses, the descendants of Jacob, known as the Israelites,
flee from Egypt and head across the Sinai Desert on their way back
to the Land of Canaan. Along the way they stop at Mount Sinai,
where God reveals himself to the entire people and gives them the
Ten Commandments. Over the next forty years, Moses will give the
people additional commandments that become the basis of the Jewish
religion.

about 1020 B.C.E.
Although the Israelites have been settled in Canaan for two centuries, they are a divided people until Saul becomes their first king.

about 1000
David succeeds his father-in-law Saul as king and makes Jerusalem his capital.

960
David's son Solomon becomes king and builds the First Temple in Jerusalem. Shortly after his death, however, the kingdom is split into the Northern Kingdom of Israel, ruled by a succession of dynasties, and the Kingdom of Judah, ruled by David and Solomon's descendants.

about 800
A group of prophets begins to warn the Jewish people of an impending disaster if they abandon God, but of great glory if they observe the commandments and act mercifully to one another. Chief among these prophets is Elijah, who prophesied in the Northern Kingdom, and Isaiah, who prophesied in Judah.

722
The Northern Kingdom falls to the Assyrian empire and its people are led into exile, never to be heard from again.

about 620
King Josiah attempts to restore the ancient religion and cleanses the Temple. In the process, he finds an ancient scroll, which is verified by the prophetess Huldah as a lost book of the Bible, the Book of Deuteronomy.

586
The Kingdom of Judah falls to the Babylonian empire. The Temple in Jerusalem is destroyed, and the people are led into exile in Babylonia.

538 B.C.E.
King Cyrus of Persia, who conquered the Babylonians, allows the exiles from Judah, now known as Jews, to return to their homes and rebuild their Temple.

515
The construction of the Second Temple is completed.

450–400
Two leaders, Ezra and Nehemiah, launch a religious reform and codify the first five books of the Bible.

about 333
The armies of Alexander the Great conquer Jerusalem and introduce Greek culture to the Jews.

168
The Jews revolt against the imposition of Greek culture by King Antiochus IV Epiphanes. They take control of the Temple and relight the menorah, or ancient candelabrum, marked by Jews today as the festival of Hanukkah. The descendants of the rebels establish a Jewish kingdom called Judea, which soon finds itself supported by Rome.

63
The Romans under Pompey annex Judea.

about 10
Herod dedicates a magnificently restored Temple, which is considered by many to be an architectural wonder of the times. Hillel and Shammai are the two great religious leaders of the era.

70 C.E.
After a four-year revolt by the Jews against Roman rule, the Romans occupy Jerusalem and destroy the Temple. Without the Temple, the synagogue and study hall become the centers of Jewish life.

135 C.E.
After another failed revolt by the Jews, the Romans destroy Jerusalem again, and forbid Jews entry to the city.

150
The selection of the books that will form the Jewish Bible is completed by the rabbis of Jamniah.

200
Rabbi Judah Ha-Nasi completes the Mishna, a codification of religious laws that becomes the basis of the Talmud.

359
Hillel II, a descendant of Hillel, formalizes the Jewish calendar.

400
A first version of the Talmud is completed in northern Israel. It is known as the Jerusalem Talmud out of reverence for the city.

600
A second version of the Talmud, known as the Babylonian Talmud, is completed in the Jewish academies of Babylonia, particularly in Sura, Pumpeditha, and Nehardea.

638
Muslim troops under Omar conquer Jerusalem and allow the Jews to return to the city. By now, however, Jews are scattered throughout the Middle East and around the Mediterranean.

1040–1150
Rabbi Solomon Yitzchaki, known by the Hebrew acronym Rashi, completes a monumental commentary on the Bible and the Talmud, in the city of Worms.

1135–1204
Maimonides, a Jewish physician and scholar living in Egypt, codifies all of Jewish law in fourteen volumes.

1200s

The Zohar, the primary book of Jewish mysticism, begins being circulated in Spain. Within decades, it has spread throughout most of the Jewish world.

1290

The Jews are expelled from England.

1492

Ferdinand and Isabella complete the Christian conquest of Spain and force the sizable Jewish population either to convert to Catholicism or leave the country.

1516

The Jews of Venice are barred from living anywhere but in a specific neighborhood of the city, which became known as the ghetto. Over the next few centuries, ghettos will be created for Jews throughout much of central Europe.

1567–1571

Rabbi Joseph Karo publishes his *Code of Jewish Law*, still the authoritative text on Jewish practice for Orthodox Jews.

1648–1649

Many of the Jewish communities in Poland and the Ukraine are destroyed during the Cossack Uprising, led by Bogdan Chmielnicki.

1654

Jews settle in New Amsterdam, now New York, establishing the first Jewish community in what would become the United States. The following year, Oliver Cromwell allows Jews to return to England.

1656

The Jewish philosopher Benedict Spinoza is excommunicated for heresy by the Jewish community of Amsterdam.

1700–1760

Rabbi Israel Baal Shem Tov, a Jewish mystic, preaches that God should be served through worship and song. His followers, known as the Hassidim, are the ancestors of the modern hassidic community of Jews.

1779

Thomas Jefferson writes the Virginia Statute for Religious Freedom, the first formal document to grant Jews equality with their neighbors. It was echoed in the First Amendment to the U.S. Constitution, which was ratified in 1791.

1729–1786

Moses Mendelssohn, a Jewish scholar, calls on Jews to embrace the Enlightenment and on the German leadership to accept the Jews as full citizens.

1810–1874

Rabbi Abraham Geiger teaches that Judaism is an evolving religion, laying the foundation for Reform Judaism.

1873

Reform Jews establish the Union of American Hebrew Congregations in the United States.

1880–1923

Two and a half million Jews leave the major Jewish population centers in eastern Europe for the United States.

1886

Conservative Jews found the Jewish Theological Seminary in the United States.

1896

Theodor Herzl publishes *The Jewish State*, founding the Zionist movement, which calls for the establishment of an independent Jewish homeland.

1909

Tel Aviv, the first Hebrew-speaking city in almost two thousand years, is founded.

1935

Jews in Germany are stripped of their rights by the Nazi dictator Adolf Hitler.

1939–1945

About six million European Jews are murdered by the Nazis during World War II in an event that came to be known as the Holocaust.

1948

The Jews living in Palestine are granted independence by the United Nations. They call their new country Israel. Over the next few years, they are soon joined by waves of immigrants, including survivors of the Holocaust, entire Jewish communities from around the Middle East and North Africa, as well as Jews from North and South America.

1967

During the Six Day War, Israel captures the Old City of Jerusalem.

1972

The Reform movement in the United States ordains the first woman rabbi.

GLOSSARY

aliyah—A ritual in the synagogue in which a person is called up to the Torah scroll to make a blessing over it, before and after it is read. Aliyah literally means "going up."

anti-Semitism—Hatred of Jews and Judaism, often leading to terrible persecution. Jews have faced many difficult periods of anti-Semitism throughout their history, recently during the Holocaust in Europe.

aravot—Willow branches, used during the synagogue service during the holiday of Sukkot.

Ashkenazim—Jews whose ancestors lived in Europe.

bal tashchit—The commandment not to waste anything, including food, paper, or natural resources.

bar mitzvah—A ceremony in which a young Jewish man comes of age and assumes responsibility as part of the Jewish community. It occurs when a boy is thirteen years old.

bat mitzvah—A modern ceremony for young Jewish women that is similar to the bar mitzvah ceremony. It occurs when a girl is twelve or thirteen years old.

brachah—A short prayer, especially the prayer said before eating.

challah—A twisted loaf of rich bread, traditionally served on the Sabbath and holidays.

charoset—A sweet paste of apples, nuts, wine, and spices, eaten with *marror* during the seder to take away some of the bitterness.

Chol HaMoed—The middle days of the holidays of Sukkot and Passover. Work may be performed during *Chol HaMoed*, but other commandments relating to the holiday and its prayer services still apply.

chulent—A rich stew, often served for lunch on the Sabbath.

chuppah—A canopy, under which the bride and groom stand during a traditional Jewish wedding ceremony. The *chuppah* represents the home they will build together.

circumcision—An operation performed on Jewish baby boys when they are eight days old, in which the foreskin is removed. Circumcision, called a *brit* in Hebrew, marks the covenant that God made with Abraham.

confirmation—A ceremony held by Reform and many Conservative Jews for young Jewish men and women to mark their adolescence. It is often celebrated on the holiday of Shavuot.

Conservative Jews—Jews who follow the traditional commandments, but believe that the teachings of the rabbis should evolve to reflect modern times.

etrog—A citron fruit, used during the synagogue service during the holiday of Sukkot.

Grace after Meals—A prayer said upon completing a meal in which bread was served.

Hachnasat orchim—Welcoming guests, one of the important commandments of Judaism.

hadasim—Myrtle branches used during the synagogue service during the holiday of Sukkot.

haftorah—A reading from the prophets that follows the reading from the Torah on the Sabbath and holidays.

Haggadah—A book telling the story of the Exodus from Egypt, which is read during the Passover seder.

Hanukkah—An eight-day festival celebrated in mid-winter to commemorate the Jews' victory over the Syrian Greeks in a struggle for religious freedom. It is customary to light candles in a menorah set in the window.

Hassidic Jews—A group of Orthodox Jews who follows the teachings of Rabbi Israel Baal Shem Tov and believes that the way to come closest to God is through a life devoted to worship and celebration.

havdalah—A brief prayer said over wine, spices, and a flame, to mark the end of the Sabbath.

hazzan—The cantor who leads the prayer service in many synagogues.

Hebrew—The language spoken by the Jews in ancient times. It survived as the language of Jewish prayer and writing, and in its modern form is now the official language of the State of Israel.

Holocaust—The calculated mass murder of the Jewish people and others in Europe under the Nazi regime, which occurred during World War II. About six million Jews were killed in the Holocaust.

Holy Ark—A cupboard in the synagogue where the Torah scrolls are kept.

Jerusalem—The city in Israel where the Jewish people once had its Temple. Jerusalem is still considered to be the holy city of the Jewish people.

Kabbalat Shabbat—A joyful service recited before *ma'ariv* on Friday evening to welcome the Sabbath.

kaddish—A prayer praising God, which is often recited by mourners during the first eleven months after the death of a parent or loved one and on occasion thereafter.

ketubah—A Jewish wedding document, signed beneath the *chuppah* during a marriage service.

kiddush—A prayer said over wine before festive meals on Shabbat and the holidays.

Kol Nidrei—The opening service on Yom Kippur, in which people ask to be released from any vows they made during the year.

kosher—Food that is permitted to be eaten according to the Torah. The Jewish dietary laws are called kashrut.

lulav—A palm branch, used during the synagogue service during the holiday of Sukkot.

ma'ariv—The evening prayer service.

maftir—The final reading from the Torah on the Sabbath and holidays.

Magen David—The star of David, a six-pointed star that is a symbol of Judaism.

Mahzor—A Jewish prayerbook for the holidays.

marror—Bitter herbs, eaten during the Passover seder to remember the bitterness of slavery in Egypt.

matzo—A crackerlike bread served instead of challah during the holiday of Passover to remind Jews of the unleavened bread they ate in Egypt and during the Exodus.

mazal tov—Literally "good luck," a Hebrew phrase commonly used to wish people congratulations on happy occasions.

menorah—A candelabrum, most famously the one used in the Temple, but now found in many synagogues. Traditionally, the menorah has seven branches, but on Hannukah a menorah with eight branches is lit in Jewish homes to celebrate the holiday.

Messiah—In Jewish tradition, a righteous person who will lead the Jewish people back to their ancient homeland and institute an era of peace for all humanity. Many Jews believe that this is a metaphor for a time of peace and happiness for all humanity that will one day occur.

mezuzah—A case containing a small parchment scroll with the Shema, which is hung on the doorposts of a Jewish home.

Minchah—The afternoon prayer service.

mitzvah—A commandment in the Torah. Traditionally, there are 613 different commandments.

Mizrahim—Jews whose ancestors lived in the Middle East and North Africa.

musaf—A special prayer service recited on Sabbath and the holidays.

Neilah—The concluding prayer service of Yom Kippur.

Orthodox Jews—Jews who follow the commandments most strictly, according to the traditional interpretations of the rabbis.

pareve—Food that is not considered either meat or dairy according to Jewish law. All fruits and vegetables are pareve.

Parsha—A weekly reading of the Torah.

Pesach (**Passover**)—A holiday, celebrated in the spring, to mark the Exodus of the Jews from Egypt.

Pharisees—During the time of the Second Temple, Jews who believed that the laws of the Torah should be interpreted by the rabbis.

priest—In ancient times, a member of the extended family that served in the Temple in Jerusalem. The Hebrew word for priest is *Cohen*.

Purim—A festival in late winter to celebrate how a decree against the Jews was abolished in the days of the Persian empire.

rabbi—A member of the Jewish clergy. Rabbis are literally teachers, though they often lead the service in the synagogue.

Reconstructionist Jews—Jews who believe that Judaism is not just a religion but also a civilization and culture.

Reform Jews—Jews who believe that Judaism is an evolving religion and that some of the commandments are no longer relevant in the modern world.

Rosh Hashanah—The Jewish New Year, celebrated in early autumn.

Sabbath—The Jewish day of rest, celebrated on Saturday. Traditionally, Jews abstain from any creative work on the Sabbath. In Hebrew, the day is called *Shabbat*.

Saduccees—During the time of the Second Temple, Jews who believed that the laws of the Torah should be observed as they appear in the Torah, without the interpretation of the rabbis.

Sanhedrin—The supreme Jewish court in the time of the Second Temple.

seder—A ritual meal, served on the first two nights of Passover.

Sephardim—Jews whose ancestors originated in Spain and Portugal. The term is sometimes used to describe all Jews who live in the Middle East and North Africa.

Shacharit—The morning prayer service.

shalom—The Hebrew word for peace. It is often used as a greeting or to say good-bye.

Shavuot—A harvest festival, also celebrating the giving of the Torah on Mount Sinai. It is celebrated seven weeks after the first day of Passover.

Shema—A Jewish prayer, recited twice every day, proclaiming belief in one God.

Shemini Atzeret-Simchat Torah—The holiday immediately following Sukkot, celebrating the completion of the reading of the Torah.

shiva—A seven-day mourning period for the family of the deceased, which begins immediately after a funeral.

Shmoneh Esrei—A prayer recited during each prayer service. It literally means the "Eighteen Benedictions," though the weekday *shmoneh esrei* has nineteen benedictions, and the ones recited on Sabbath and holidays are shorter. It is recited standing and in a whisper.

shofar—A ram's horn, blown as a trumpet during the synagogue service on Rosh Hashanah.

siddur—A Jewish prayerbook.

Sukkot—A harvest festival, celebrated five days after Yom Kippur. During Sukkot, many Jews eat their meals outdoors in a little booth called a sukkah.

synagogue—A place where Jews gather to worship and celebrate together. It is also called a *shul* in Yiddish, and a temple by Reform Jews. In Hebrew it is called a *beit knesset*.

tallith—A four-cornered shawl with tassels, called tzitzit, hanging from each corner, worn by many Jews during prayer.

Talmud—A collection of Jewish laws and stories, edited by the rabbis of Israel and Babylonia 400–600 C.E. The Talmud is the most important Jewish text written by the rabbis.

tefillin—Leather boxes bound to the arm and head with straps during the weekday morning service. The tefillin contain four tiny parchment scrolls with verses from the Torah.

Temple—A complex of buildings in Jerusalem that was the center of Jewish life in ancient times. It was where Jews gathered to worship and offer sacrifices to God. The First Temple was destroyed by the Babylonians in 586 B.C.E.; the Second Temple was destroyed by the Romans in 70 C.E. Today Reform Jews usually refer to their synagogues as temples.

tikkun olam—The belief that the role of people is to "repair the world" and make it a better place for everyone.

Tishah-b'Ab—A day of fasting in the summer that marks the destruction of both the First and Second Temples in Jerusalem.

Torah scroll—A parchment scroll containing the first five books of the Bible.

Torah—The accumulated teachings of the Jewish people, as they appear in the Bible and the writings of the rabbis.

tzaddik—A righteous person.

tzedakah—Charity, one of the most important commandments in Judaism.

tzizit—The tassels with eight strings that hang down from the corners of the tallith.

vidui—Confession, recited by the entire community as part of the prayer service. *Vidui* is traditionally recited on Rosh Hashanah and Yom Kippur, though many Jews recite it every weekday too.

yarmulke—A small cap worn by many Jewish men and some women, either all day or during prayers. In Hebrew, the yarmulke is called a *kippah*.

Yiddish—A language, closely related to German, spoken by Jews who lived in eastern Europe. Today most speakers of Yiddish live in the United States and Israel.

Yom Kippur—The Day of Atonement, a time for Jews to ask forgiveness from God and their fellow human beings. It is a day of prayer and fasting, celebrated one week after Rosh Hashanah.

FURTHER RESOURCES

There are many excellent books about Judaism that are easily available. Here are just a few:

Donin, Hayim Halevy. *To Be a Jew: A Guide to Jewish Observance in Contemporary Life.* New York: Basic Books, 1991.

Kertzer, Morris M. *What Is a Jew?* New York, Simon and Schuster, 1996.

Prager, Dennis, and Joseph Telushkin. *The Nine Questions People Ask about Judaism.* New York, Simon and Schuster, 1981.

Siegel, Richard, Michael Strassfeld, and Sharon Strassfeld. *The Jewish Catalogue.* Philadelphia: Jewish Publication Society of America, 1973.

Steinberg, Milton. *Basic Judaism.* New York, Harvest Books, 1965.

Telushkin, Joseph. *Jewish Literacy: The Most Important Things to Know about the Jewish Religion, Its People, and Its History.* New York: William Morrow and Company, 2001.

Wouk, Herman. *This Is My God.* Boston: Little Brown, 1988.

WEB SITES

There are many excellent Web sites with information about Jewish beliefs, rituals, history, and contemporary issues.

Ask a Rabbi

http://www.askarabbi.com/

Everything Jewish

http://www.everythingjewish.com/

Hanefesh Community

http://www.hanefesh.com/

A Web site with information about Judaism for college students

Introduction to Judaism

http://judaism.about.com/library/weekly/mpreviss_judaism_intro.htm

Jewish Virtual Library

http://www.jewishvirtuallibrary.org/

Frequently Asked Questions and Answers: What Is Reform Progressive Judaism?

http://www.shamash.org/lists/scj-faq/HTML/faq/02-05.html

Wikipedia, a free, online encyclopedia, (http://en.wikipedia.org), has an extensive collection of articles about Judaism from many different perspectives, as well as links to traditional Jewish sources in English. For more information, see http://en.wikipedia.org/wiki/Judaism

SOURCE NOTES

All quotes have been taken from the *Jerusalem Bible: Reader's Edition* (1968). The word *Yahweh* has been replaced by "God," and in one instance (Numbers 15:40) the text has been amended to more accurately reflect the Hebrew original.

Translations from the Prayer Book and Talmud are entirely the author's.

The transcription of terms and phrases in Hebrew and other languages posed a particular problem because of differences in pronunciation used in the various Jewish communities around the world. In general, the modern Hebrew pronunciation used in the State of Israel was adopted, with parallel Ashkenazi transliterations given alongside when deemed appropriate. This is evident mainly in the final *t* changing into an *s*, and the use of the vowel *o* instead of *a* under certain conditions.

The following vowels are pronounced as they would be in these

English words:

A is pronounced as in *father*.

E is pronounced as in *get*.

I is pronounced as in *machine*.

O is pronounced as in *go*.

U is pronounced as in *ruse*.

The diphthong *ei*, which appears in Yiddish words, is pronounced *ay* as in *day*.

G is always pronounced as in *girl*.

The combination *ch* is pronounced as in the Scottish *loch*. One exception to this rule is the Yiddish word *chulent*, in which the *ch* is pronounced as in *choose*.

INDEX
Page numbers in **boldface** are illustrations.